Godfident

Voices

One Message Through the Voices of Many

Compiled by Ilona Parunakova

Gabriel's Horn ~ 2021

Cover design: Aminum Islam Shihab

Contact editors@gabrielshornpress.com
Published Minneapolis, Minnesota
by Gabriel's Horn Press
First printing: June 2021 Printed in the United States.
ISBN-13: 978-1-938990-69-4

Table of Contents

Godfident Voices

ENDORSEMENTS

Great read with inspiring stories that show how people can turn their experiences of trauma and tragedy into strength, perseverance and never-ending personal growth. Bravo to the brave writers who are willing to be vulnerable in the face of adversity and come out the other end as heros.

Rachel Stone
Women Empowerment Coach,
Author of *Love Affair 101*

Roma's Story

ROMA FLOOD

If a life full of tragedy, trauma and grief shape someone, then I should be a well-rounded person. On meeting me at a restaurant, a friend described me as follows: a well-groomed lady of Chinese descent; tall, thin and poised, perhaps even serene. What she could not see or even guess at, was the suffering and loss I have endured. Too much for any one lifetime.

My suffering began in my teenage years with my precious mother's illness and death due to ovarian cancer. I was sixteen years old and my mum meant the world to me. Dad was rarely around, usually drowning his sorrows at the local pub and his presence was sorely missed at the most needed time in my life. After my mother's funeral, whilst on holidays with a girlfriend I received an unexpected phone call from my father to say that I was to live with my aunty and uncle when I returned home as he was leaving at that very moment to live back in the city. I felt numb with the turn of events. I felt grief-stricken and abandoned.

Two years later I married Bernard and had two

children, a daughter Danielle and a son Jamie. Danielle's teenage years proved to be quite turbulent, leading her into the drug scene. We experienced many a night not knowing where she was. She partnered with a young man who was also on drugs and they had two children. The relationship ended with Danielle taking the children away for a holiday. However, due to a series of events she stayed in a women's refuge where she was brutally murdered in the middle of the night and her two children kidnapped by the murderer.

I know Danielle walked into the enemy's camp, a place she never should have ventured. The abrasion of darkness and light was very evident in that place and due to the immense battle in the spiritual realm. My daughter was martyred for the kingdom. A martyr is a witness or advocate for Christ and her new-found love for Jesus was evident in a new Bible she had just purchased, filled with written scripture. The enemy viciously and brutally robbed her of her precious young life; a young mother ripped from the arms of her children and for me a daughter no more. The enemy did what he does best: robbed, stole, and destroyed that which was beautiful.

The children's well-being and security being our first priority, my husband Bernard and I proudly raised Danielle's children as our own. Ten years later I was taking a short walk as my husband and grandchildren were going to go to the park and play ball. As I was walking, a quick flash of the checkered pattern on a police car crossed my mind. I shook my head, discounting it as ridiculous and kept walking. Unfortunately, the vision I had was true, for as I walked up my driveway a police car was parked there and the policeman came out of the house with bad news yet again. My granddaughter Lysinda, age thirteen, and my husband were both killed in a freak plane crash. It was too much pain for one body to contain.

If you look at me across the table, you would never guess at the rawness and grief that have ravaged me. I have lived everyone's worst nightmares, their greatest fears, but I have survived each and every one. Through the days and nights, weeks and years I never thought I could live through, I discovered that the power of love, unfaltering relationships, and immovable faith can overcome the most gut-wrenching experiences imaginable. I am a Christian and am not afraid to tell you because my life is just like yours–full of guaranteed challenges, anxiety, hardship and profound loss. My story is unique; however the keys to recovery are available to all who have experienced some form of hardship, loss or grief in their lives. Everyone will find something for themselves in my journey. This is a story of resilience, recovery and restoration.

I became a Christian while Danielle was on drugs and the family unit was in disarray. Let me dispel the myth that if you are a Christian, grief doesn't hurt because you have faith. The reality is we are all the same, made of flesh and blood, and we all have a soul. We are frail and weak and without strength and hope if we don't have Jesus in our lives.

My life is raw and real and I don't try to hide my frailty and flaws because it shows how far I have come because of Him. Yes, I went through all the stages of grief: shock, anger, disillusionment, withdrawal. Panic attacks and loss of security encompassed me after Danielle's death.

As I just started to enjoy and live life again after her death, the shock of losing both my husband and grand-daughter in the plane crash was harrowing and caused me to spiral. I had a business to run. Staff problems compounded the anxiety, causing me to fight to survive each day, but I had a choice: I could get better or bitter.

In life, pain is inevitable, but misery is optional. The more I pursued peace, the easier each day became, but let me assure you I had to intentionally pursue it. I had to fight to protect what was important. Pursuing peace takes persistence and a lot of resistance. We have the choice as to whether we allow the battle to rage in our minds or instead cut off the negative thoughts that pull us down into the mud. You have the inherent strength to dis-empower every thought. The effect of doing that determines your day—to utterly destroy it or utterly enjoy it. Get hostile and tell the negative thoughts to shut up. Once you are free on the inside, you will walk free on the outside. Stinking thinking will affect you psychologically and physically. It will not change your circumstances but it will affect you. So step back. Step away from the problem and remember who is important. You!

It simply starts in your imagination. By the act of seeing, you start believing. Every time you give time and energy to negative thoughts, you empower them and that is a complete waste of time and contrary to your desired outcome. Start to look through a faith-filled lens and see a good outcome. Observation will bring transformation.

Don't befriend your fear and brokenness. Contend for your freedom and wholeness. You can be the architect of your day and success. Set your resolve and purpose to be a fearless over-comer. Your outward actions will not change if your inward actions are not positioned for success, so I looked for the good. I made a decisive choice to not allow my past hardships and failures dictate my future. How we navigate each problem is our choice. It's also our choice as to how or what we say about the problem. Our thoughts are the culprits that keep us captive and bound for longer than we should, but essentially we give them permission to do so. So change your thinking and your words will change. The outcome from this adjustment will certainly relieve your stress levels and enable you to be less consumed with the taxing circumstances, resulting in a more peaceful you.

Stay in today. Today has enough problems of its own without going back over and over what has happened in the past. Before you go to sleep tonight, establish that as soon as you open your eyes tomorrow, you will make a conscious effort to think on that for which you are thankful. It is impossible to think a good and bad thought at the same time. Better to think of the good, or the grief will certainly fill that void. Your first thought in the morning can position you for the rest of your day.

No one has more influence in your life than yourself. So, what does your self-talk sound like? If your confession aligns with your circumstances, you will never step into your destiny.

Self-prophesy and positive affirmation statements will change your thinking which changes your actions and pulls you out of the pit. A transformed mind and attitude puts you on the winner's podium.

Fear and timidity may have caused you to shut down and lose confidence. Fear will attack what you are afraid to lose. It's time to determine that you will not let a temporary emotion keep you from an amazing future. Even though you feel battle-weary, start to encourage yourself and look for the good in each day. Grief does not have to be a life sentence. It does have an expiry date.

Embarking on the journey of forgiveness is something I chose to do so that I could become healed and whole. Speaking the words out loud validates them and gives them form and credibility. If you make the decision that the offense will not dictate to you, then the act of forgiveness restores the power back into your hands. So forgive them and let it go. When I forgave Danielle's murderer, I did it by denying her the victory over my emotions, by not staying bitter, and by letting go.

Don't live with regrets. Regret is like a parasite that eats away at your mind and your strength. Don't nurse it, don't rehearse it, take action and reverse it. Know that God is not to blame.

Let truth extinguish the flame of unbelief.

Hope does not disappoint but keeps one focused on the outcome. It kept me steadfast and stable. Far better to be a prisoner of hope than a prisoner of doubt and unbelief, so unlock your door to a vast world of faith and belief. Seeing is believing.

Know this: there is no 'one size fits all' grieving process. We are all individuals with different character traits and there are many variables surrounding a loss of any type in general. So, be kind to yourself and breathe.

Grief and loss cause us to be introspective, but when we look to do something for someone else, amazingly we are the ones who reap the benefits.

Tragedy doesn't have to be the end, nor does it say

that once touched by it you will never recover. My being vulnerable didn't break me because it is for others to break through. I pray that through my adversity and grief and the strategies God has so graciously equipped me with to walk in freedom and wholeness, that you, too, may utilize them daily to enable you to also walk in freedom. But don't forget this one thing: without Jesus, my life-source and inspiration, I would not be where I am today. Fall into Him for He will sustain you. He will guide you. He will strengthen you. He will heal you. His love and thoughts toward you exceed the number of grains of sand on the sea-shore. That is the immense love He has for you. Take a step toward Him and receive it today.

Roma Flood
Author of *Despite the Odds*
Diploma of Teaching Technical
Australia

Persistence against Adversity

DR. RENCI DENHAM

I was born in 1961 in the hills of Pennsylvania. We were poor. I remember one time we went to visit a relative who lived in the housing projects and I said, "Wow! You must be rich! You have running water, a bathtub, and heat!" My mother was a sometime factory worker. She was a fundamentalist Christian and an extreme hypocrite who had numerous affairs. She frequently sat me and my siblings on our "uncles'" laps so they could hug and kiss us in exchange for 20 dollars. At eight, she sent me to a relative's house daily to clean and cook for him. When I told her what my other duties were, she said, "We need the three dollars a night he pays you. Without that money we would all starve. Just make sure you're a virgin so you don't bring shame down upon us."

My bipolar father beat me regularly. He used a belt, a paddle from a butter churn, a shoe—whatever instrument of torture he could grab. When he died when I was 12, I cried at the funeral because I knew only a "bad" girl would not mourn the loss of a parent. I knew I must have been a "bad" girl but I did not want the world to see how "bad" I was.

Three weeks later, my mother's best friend's husband moved in and began sharing a bed with her. Her friend came to the house to confront her. My mother's friend said, "Margaret, I know he's living here. Please just be honest with me!"

"No he's not Betty. I don't know why you think he's living here. He's not!"

"Margaret, I can see the shoes I bought him sitting right there in the corner. I've watched him come here and stay. Please just be honest with me."

"No he's not Betty! I'm a good Christian woman! I would not commit adultery or lie."

I looked at Betty, at my mother, and back to Betty. I knew there would be hell to pay later if I said anything but I had to speak up. "Betty, he is living here."

Betty looked at me and said, "Thank you, Florence."

My mother of course was livid. "You're imagining things Florence! You're as crazy as your father."

My mother's boyfriend "Pappy" stayed. When it was time for me to go clean the relatives' house he looked at my mother and said, "Margaret, let the girl be a kid. She needs to go out and have fun. Here's 80 dollars. Go buy her some decent clothes to wear to school. She looks like a ragamuffin!"

For the next five years, my life was as normal as I had ever known it. I went to school, I made friends, I even went to my junior prom. One day when I was a senior in high school, my life changed forever. I had a sharp pain in my stomach and began throwing up. My parents took me to the hospital. It was indeed bad news. My appendix had ruptured and yes, I was pregnant. *Not good!*

Pappy looked at me and said, "So you're pregnant. Even a dog doesn't give their babies away and neither will you. We'll keep it and raise it." My mother was not as supportive.

I graduated high school and went to college. It was not by any means easy. When other students were at parties, I was up with a colicky baby. However, I did it—I graduated!

A year later, I was married to an old high school friend. Unemployment was astronomical in western Pennsylvania so we moved to Virginia. We were young and we struggled. Soon we took a job as house parents in a group home. We lived there with three children for 9,000 dollars a year. The day before Thanksgiving a social worker called. "We'll be picking up the kids in an hour."

I said, "What are you talking about? Tomorrow is Thanksgiving."

The voice on the phone went silent and then said,

"Don't you know?"

"Know what?"

The social worker responded, "The owner of the company stole all the money. You have to be out of that house in three days."

Tiwanna and Johnny were picked up at school; I did not get to say goodbye. Antwan's social worker brought Antwan by the house. She had adoption papers for us to sign.

I looked at her and said, "We are 23, unemployed and homeless. I love him but I can't adopt him." I burst into tears, and looked at Antwan. "I am so sorry. If we had more time—but we don't even have a job or a place to live ourselves."

Antwan hugged me and said, "I understand, Mom." I don't think he really did.

Years went by. We struggled until we both got decent jobs. We bought a house. It was ugly, but we worked hard to make it nice. We bought new cars, went out to dinner and plays. One day I was at work and the phone rang. I picked it up. "Residential Service, how can I help you?"

The voice on the other end said, "Florence, I'm at the hospital with Mike. A balcony collapsed on him. He's alive but he's hurt. We need you to come right away."

Mike had ruptured three disks, and been unconscious for an unknown amount of time. His back would never be the same. For several months, workman's comp covered the bills—and then they stopped. "Not work related," they said. We had to live on one income.

The next two years were hell. My husband began to drink and use drugs to dull the pain. He became aggressive. I couldn't take it anymore. I went to the women's shelter with my daughter in tow and knocked on the door. "Any room in the inn?" I asked.

We stayed at the shelter for two months. I remember one counselor said to me, "You are so much luckier than these other women. You have a good job. They're all on welfare."

I looked at her and said, "Luck had nothing to do with it. I worked very hard to get where I am."

One weekend I was visiting my parents. Out of nowhere, my stepfather fell as he was exiting his truck. He had a brain tumor the size of a grapefruit. My mother tried to put him in a home. I said "No!" I moved in with them. so that I could care for him the way he had cared for me. He died at 10:30 in the morning on December 25.

I went back home. I then met my second husband Steve and moved to St. Louis.

There, I developed a sinus infection—something that had begun to plague me—so my doctor sent me for a CAT scan. It showed chronic sinus infections but was clear now. I had more headaches, so my doctor prescribed antidepressants. When the headaches continued, he prescribed another anti-depressant and told me I must be menopausal and should go buy something pretty.

I went to the dentist for routine care. He took an x-ray. He turned to me and said, "You seem to be a pretty smart woman. I need to show you something. This black spot here, that's bad. Really bad. It shows an infection in the bone. I've never seen one this big. You need to have it cut out."

Over the next 10 years I went to Saint Louis University, Saint Mary's. and even the Mayo. Several doctors even said, "I don't know what that thing was but it went the whole way up the bridge of your nose and behind your eye." They cut it out and it would grow back. I could no longer walk without the use of a cane. I was partially blind in my right eye. I lost my sense of taste and smell—as well as my job. I was now using a walker. I finished my masters but was soon in a wheelchair.

Several years went by and we moved to Michigan. I had a new family practitioner. I told him my history.

He looked at my latest x-ray and said, "Has anyone ever stuck a needle in there and extracted the fluid to analyze it?"

I said "I have *begged* other doctors to do that and they said it couldn't be done."

He looked at me and said, "You want to do it. I can't use anesthesia but if you're willing, I'm willing."

I smiled. "Do it!"

I opened my mouth, he lifted my upper lip and stuck the needle in. We could hear the bone crunching. He pushed the needle in further and I swore like a sailor on shore leave in a cat house.

I heard him exclaim, "Oh my God! It's blood! You're hemorrhaging into your skull!"

Several months later I was sitting in the office of a neurosurgeon. I had an incredibly rare kind of tumor. However, he thought he could treat it. If I was willing, he would treat me with his very radical, very experimental procedure. He looked at me sympathetically and said, "I can't cure you. There is no cure, but I can improve your quality of life. Do you want to move forward?"

I jumped out of my chair, tripped and fell, then pushed myself up and hugged him.

Five procedures and two years later, I still had a lot of pain, but not nearly as much. I could see, smell, and walk again. I started an online PhD program. I could hold a paintbrush and paint. I bought a new car and started to drive.

Marriage is tough even in the best of times and with my health problems, marriage was even more difficult. Our house was a duplex and we split it up—me in one half and Steve in the other. I had completed the coursework for my PhD and passed my comps. I began work on my dissertation. My health started to decline again. But I was determined to move on. We still had our house in St. Louis, and I moved back by myself. My health continued to rapidly decline. I was only there for a few weeks when I became too ill to move. Steve called me and said, "You don't have to love me but please don't lay in that house and die alone. I'll take care of you. You don't have to love me but please come home."

I went home. It took a long time, but we put our marriage back together. I finished my dissertation and yes, I am now Dr. Renci Denham. Steve took me to more doctors. A bacterial and viral infection was under the dermas of my face and masses of scar tissue were gluing my face to itself and keeping the infection from draining. There was a large hole in my skull where the tumor had been. I had more surgery to fill in the hole in my skull and injections to break up the scar tissue.

The infection started to drain. It also spread throughout my body and I went septic. I was unable to walk due to crippling pain in my back and stomach. I went to the emergency room. The surgeon had to get special permission from the state government as due to the pandemic all "elective procedures" had been stopped. He was able to get me into emergency surgery the next day. He removed two benign tumors and discovered my uterus was filled with varicose veins. He said, "This is above my pay grade," and refereed me to the University of Michigan for more surgery. My team realized my problems were systemic and I was diagnosed with a rare genetic disorder called Ehlors-Danlos Syndrome. It is a connective disorder in which joints pop out of the socket, infections are difficult to fight, and, as in my case, there can be vascular malformations that can rupture.

So here I am, waiting for surgery, going to physical therapy, and getting painful injections to help my body heal the connective tissue and break up the scar tissue. I thank the Dear Lord every day for my Steve as I am completely bedridden. The only thing that separates me from one of those poor souls lying in a tent in a homeless camp dying of a drug overdose trying to stop the pain is that I have a husband who loves me.

When you see yourself judging someone just remember but for the grace of God go you or I.

Dr. Renci Denham
M.A.T., Ph.D.
United States

My Life's Expectations

DON SEVCIK

"Life is largely a matter of expectation." - Horace

I'm sitting in a cold basement, head in hands, with a knot in my stomach, trying to figure out what to do next.

You see, I built my math website as a search engine for calculators. For six years, our traffic grew. After spending six years building a website, I smacked full force into a brick wall. Traffic plateaued, people stopped promoting us, and my dream fizzled out. Each time I sat down at the computer in my office, it smelled like failure.

To get to the next level, I had to figure out how to do something I'd never done before. I had to figure out how to do something many told me was impossible. "You'd have better odds trying to cure cancer," somebody told me.

And this obstacle taught me my first lesson…

You must create a positivity force field around you. When you start your quest for a big goal in life, your first obstacles arrive quickly. They're disguised as friends, colleagues, and sometimes, even family telling you all the reasons you can't make your goal.

To achieve your goal, your positivity force field must be on full power at all times. Otherwise, the doubters and naysayers will drag you down into the pit of mediocrity. You must conquer this enemy before you start your quest. Then, and only then, can you start marching toward your prize. This is how my journey to jump a nasty hurdle in my business began.

For the first six years, people asked for concepts, like "algebra" or "equation" or "division." But now, they wanted to run their math problems directly. They asked for $2x - 9 = 31$ or the sum of the first 25 odd numbers. When my site couldn't handle the way they asked for math problems, they left immediately. This is why my traffic numbers froze like a deer in headlights.

In order to grow, I had to figure this out. I spun my wheels for two weeks. Then I remembered a key lesson I learned in my second year building my website. I took this straight out of *Think and Grow Rich:* the power of visualization and desire combined.

When I first built my website, I'd solve problems using my subconscious. I used Romans 4:17: "*Even* God, who quickeneth the dead, and calleth those things which be not as though they were."

You see, to solve my problems, I'd take a picture of the problem and imagine a solution. I'd fall asleep assuming the solution would arrive. And during my sleep or when I'd wake up, the solution popped into my mind. I kept a notepad and pen by my bed to catch these visions on paper when I was in slumber mode. First a thought, then a thing.

The key to solving my problems used a combination of Romans 4:17 and the famous Roman poet Horace's quote about Life: "Life is largely a matter of expectation."

As I lay down to sleep, I imagined in one hand my problem, and in the other my solution, and in my mind, I'd hold a vision of *expecting* the solution.

Every answer we seek must be created in our mind first. We must hold the vision and the expectation and keep it before us. This is what I did.

I imagined my website in the future, where it could answer math problems of any kind directly. I imagined I had the skills to build this. I fell asleep each night with these expectations.

This is the power of Romans 4:17: Creation through manifestation. Once you realize the power of being a Creator, your life will change. If you pay attention, you see this phenomenon referenced in pop psychology and science.

- The Holy Spirit is equivalent to The Force in Star Wars
- In science, we know it as the quantum field

As you see the vision and believe in it with full conviction, the answer arrives. After two weeks of holding the vision before me, my answer did arrive. By chance, I caught up with an old friend for drinks. My friend had a brilliant mind for programming, so I presented my problem to him. Like a wise shepherd guiding his flock, he pointed me in the right direction.

He spoke one word which changed the course of my destiny: Regex.

For the next week, I digested anything I could about Regex. I ate, breathed, and slept regex. And it paid off. Regex gave me the power to understand how people ask for math help. Regex deals with patterns. Since people have a few ways of saying the same thing, all I had to do was recognize how they asked for something, and I'd know *what they wanted.*

But I hit another wall shortly after. How would I know what patterns to look for? It would take decades to figure out how many different ways people ask for math problems. After swallowing a big glass of humility, I decided to return to my original strategy. I'd let my subconscious mind help me.

So I fell asleep the next night with my problem in hand and my expectation of a solution. I'd let Romans 4:17 guide me, calling on things unseen as though they were already here. During the night, about 3:56 AM, the answer came to me in my sleep. I slowly rolled out of bed and wrote it on my notepad.

Google has a tool called Google Analytics which helps you get intelligence on your website visitors, like age, country, and devices used on your site. My dream told me to let them come to me, meaning, let the users tell me what they want. You see, Google Analytics has a special tool called an internal search monitor. You install this and it records any search run on a website search engine.

If I recorded the searches, I'd know *how* people ask for math problems. The internal search report solved my traffic plateau problem. Once I knew the three or four ways people ask for a certain math problem, I'd program the patterns and point them to the correct calculator. Users would love it, they'd stay longer, and they'd refer more people.

It turns out this little fix, created out of thin air in my subconscious, gave me the key to unlock my destiny. In 2019, we got 3.8 million unique visitors. In 2020, at the time of this writing, we're on pace to get 5 million unique visitors. Most of our users ask for their problem directly because of this subconscious savior.

And it's all thanks to the principle which sold 100 million copies of *Think and Grow Rich* and made the Bible the most read book of all time. We have the power to create and alter our destiny. It starts as a seed planted in our mind, and it grows into an idea. The idea, with desire and focus, transforms into a manifested reality you can reach out and touch.

I can't promote this power enough. Each and every one of us has it. Write down *one clear desire you have*. You must state this as a positive command with the perception that you already have your wish. Here's an example:

I have $100,000 in my bank account.

Once you have your positive command, you meditate for at least 15 minutes per day on this desire. You fall asleep with this desire clear in your mind as you drift off to sleep. Rinse and repeat daily and you'll find the Master Key to Your Desire.

Don Sevcik
Founder and Creator of MathCelebrity, an automated online math tutor, which in 2019, tutored 3.81 million students and parents.
Author of *Free Traffic Frenzy* and *One Second Math*.
United States

Time is the Essence

DR. RAHIL KHAN

I never knew I had that much strength to fight at the same time on so many fronts. My first fight was within myself, to fight for my identity; then to struggle for education and search for my career path, as I was still not focused on what to do with my life; and finally to carry the responsibilities of all my dependents. At the age of 29, that included my parents, an aunt, three younger siblings, and my wife of barely two weeks.

During these fighting phases I sank into depression and began to feel as if I was alive but with no joy, no animation, and no hope. I was alive—but not really living. With a friend's support I found my career path, and I was happy that my working passion and hours were taking my career toward better prospects, though, it seemed, at the cost of my health. As my health seemed to grow worse, I finally went to the hospital. A series of tests revealed that the health issues were not a result of over-work and exhaustion. Rather, they were the signs of second stage cancer—Hodgkin's lymphoma.

"You are suffering with advanced stage cancer," is a statement which can shake anyone deeply, especially when he hears this from his doctor.

My reaction to hearing these five words is beyond description. I felt numb head-to-toe, and a wave of submissive humility and a crushing weight of the knowledge of so many things I had to do—and so little time left. I was just getting going in my career. I was only 15 days married! I wanted to bow down to the Divine to plead for my life.

It felt to me as if the doctor announced my diagnosis not as a doctor, but as a Supreme Court Judge, as I stood in her court. She didn't so much declare my disease as hand down capital punishment: *"You will be hanged to death."* The moment I heard her announcement, the smell of graveyard mud in the rainy season mingled with my inhaled air. It seemed the chapter of my life had ended.

I came out of the doctor's office, unable to walk even a few steps without stopping to rest. I felt the whisper of death, with echoes coming from inside myself: "You are going to die, you are going to die, you are going to die...."

Should I have taken action sooner? Should I have seen it coming? A painless node had been growing on the right side of my neck for the previous three years. In the six months before the diagnosis, I had developed fatigue, fever, night sweat, and loss of appetite. I'd begun to lose weight rapidly. As my condition had gone from bad to worst during those months, I hadn't understood why I was feeling so bad, but I had been sure that at this young age I couldn't have any serious problem. And yet, here I was.

On a breezy evening of September 5th, 2005, I went to another oncologist for a second opinion, with a ray of hope that this new doctor would declare me fit and all the earlier test reports wrong. It was a vain hope, shattered when my second-opinion-doctor advised me to go to Mumbai or London immediately, without wasting a single moment. This doctor wanted to remove the lump in my neck for closer examination.

Back at home, I struggled for the words to explain this to my family. My lips refused to articulate, my limbs were out of my command, and I couldn't find the courage to look in their eyes. When I imagined their reactions, I lost my nerve, retreated to the wash room and cried. Every moment that passed was like an ice cube melting on a plate—my life disappearing.

I had never given much care to *time*. I used to think life is a long, a very long journey, but now I realized that time is the most precious thing we have, and a thing that can end at any moment. It is out of our control. Every single dissolving-moment slipping out of my life suddenly became very precious. I wanted to stop those melting seconds, that were rolling fast and disappearing. If it were in my control, I would have stopped breathing and saved the moments of my life. Wasn't there anyone who could halt *Time* for me? Wasn't there anyone who could take this disease out of my body?

I started thinking what would happen to all my family members left behind when my soul departed from this planet. What would become of my new wife, my parents and aunt and younger brothers and sister? Next moment, my thoughts would turn to what would happen in the life Hereafter, as I had been so busy in this monetary world and hadn't earn any *'Credits'* for my last journey.

Suddenly I had everything but time—hours passed like minutes and minutes rolled by in seconds. I wanted to halt these melting moments and carry out my pending works quickly, to arrange for my family's livelihood.

The slide show of life reeled in front of my eyes, from the time of my childhood till the present moment I was breathing in. The smooth path of life seemed about to end. *How cruel those moments were!*

I arranged to go to Mumbai immediately. I arrived there the morning of September 7th, 2005 and had an appointment with the doctor that afternoon. Doctor Kamran examined me and advised me to undergo a CT scan, CBC, bone marrow, ECG, HIV, and other tests.

After the tests, the lab technician made no comment as he checked my reports, but threw a pitiful look at me. My curiosity heightened to breathlessness, ready to hear ever worse news, but he revealed nothing.

When I received all the reports in my hand, I started crying, crying, and crying—for more than half an hour, I cried. I wasn't afraid of any challenge in life. But this disease was usually incurable, and I knew, given my symptoms, and how sick I was, that the doctors were right: I had advanced cancer. I knew for sure I was going to die. I again fell to sobbing as no one was there who I could share my feelings with.

There was a chance, the doctor told me, in removing the lump in my neck. It would have to be done soon. I scheduled it and took my room in the hospital to wait. My hope was mainly in God—but I would certainly take anything the doctors offered me!

Looking out of the 6th floor of hospital, I watched the people below, their lives going on as usual, and the roads busy with traffic. Thoughts of worldly separation swung to and fro within me with strange sensations. I thought, "Nothing will ever be the same again." My belief that life was under an individual's control had been completely shattered. I had no idea what to do or how to face it.

The operation was in just a few days—but the reports said anything could happen at anytime. I badly needed my family, but decided to face the situation alone. I didn't want to know what would happen to them if they heard I had advanced stage cancer.

10ᵗʰ September 2005

The nurse wanted to call my relatives for pre-operation formalities, but as I myself was the relative and friend, I lifted the pen to sign the declaration papers with tears in my eyes. Once again negative feelings engulfed me and I felt as if I was falling into an infinitely deep black pit with no way to handle it. But as I signed the paper, a strong feeling of self-control and confidence grew within me. That was the turning point of my life.

All my pessimistic feelings were replaced with a thought: *I am ready to face everything because nothing worse than this could happen.* At the time, all pain had disappeared, and I was ready to experience everything. On the operation bed, I asked the doctor to operate in front of me as I wanted to experience everything with eyes wide open. The moment I chose to face everything, all the pains and sufferings evaporated.

During my operation, my doctor diverted my mind by asking about my college days, my family members, my hobbies, and more. In an hour, the operation was over. The doctor showed me the node which had come out of my neck. The black, bloody thing was placed in a container for further investigation.

I was taken to my hospital bed and advised to inform

my family members but at this stage of life-death dilemma I couldn't face my parents, who were very emotional and wouldn't bear such tragic news. And once again, my own emotions changed moment to moment, from despair, to horror, to hope, to extreme anger, to a state of calm.

But since I decided to face everything, my entire prospective on life had changed and given me strength to deal with all my later treatments. I underwent twelve cycles of chemotherapy and twenty-two cycles of radiotherapy. The whole process included many touching stories—like how I used that time to complete my Doctorate and further career courses with a positive feeling that *life* was back, and would be normal soon.

During my treatment, I also used to go meet other cancer patients to help them stay positive and hopeful, to help them face this challenge and encourage them to stay engaged in activities they loved.

I believe every event or incident in life has a purpose and that purpose may lead you to the next level of life or take you back to the start. You have to accept the challenge and be strong to face the situation, with more strength to fight. For big dreams, you have to be prepared for the toughest road, but trust me at the end of every struggle there is always a towering success to enjoy.

Dr. Rahil Khan,
Founder and Director for RLR Building Cleaning LLC

and Director at Work Ways Solutions LLC,
Dubai, Arab Emirates

Don't Argue
with God

LORI MAHOWALD

You could easily say of some stories, *that's no testimony,* but I would argue that God has rescued each one of us from something—even if it doesn't read as a dramatic story. In fact I would suggest that being rescued from a bland–even goodie-two shoes—life is every bit as dramatic as a rescue from a life that has been filled with tragedy.

I was raised in a God-seeking home that consisted of my mom, dad, and two sisters. My folks were born-again/saved when I was five years old and I was saved when I was eight. As the oldest sibling, I leaned toward being independent, responsible, and compliant. From the time I was in my early high school years I was working 20-40 hours a week and appreciating a lifestyle of self-reliance. I loved God and was involved in church, but as I'm honest with myself—I got more satisfaction from knowing I was exceeding expectations in my work than from my relationship with the Lord. After all, my greatest amount of time was spent working and meditating on the things of work. As much as I truly loved the Lord, work was my first love.

It was weird, however, because even though for three decades I knew God was undoubtedly the supplier of the abilities I used and the accomplishments I achieved, I was still relying on self. I consistently worked 60 to 80 or more hours a week from the time I was 22 years old until I was 52. And oddly, I was for all intents and purposes—happy! I was thankful to God for all He'd provided me, but was tickled with *myself* for being an "admirable hard-worker." Add on top of that the self-satisfaction of knowing I was a faithful tither. I was all set to continue on this path of self-satisfaction.

Then all of a sudden! What? This wasn't an "all of a sudden" type of life. In fact, I had tried diligently not to allow "all of a sudden." But it is true that it seemed like all of a sudden I realized my life wasn't as satisfying as I had tried to convince myself....*and*....I realized I was stiff-arming the Lord in the arena of my time—the dedication going to my employer. You may ask how does an "all of a sudden" occur in such a life? As Scripture says, "But God." (Ephesians 2:4-10)   Don't you love our God, who gently brings us to Himself, enriching our lives beyond what we could have ever imagined?

We were going to have a special speaker at church

and I was thinking of skipping, but my mom (who I was picking up each weekend) suggested we go even though we didn't know anything about her. Terri Savelle Foy had a message that God used to break the more than 30-year pattern in my life "all of a sudden." She spoke with such bubbly joy that was so sincere. It was foreign to me because it contained an odd mixture of peace and passion.

I knew passion—but it was in putting in tons of hours to achieve my work goals.

I knew peace—a settling I had once I knew the direction to which I was going to throw those tons of hours into my work.

I knew joy—when it was over and I exceeded the expected mark.

But to have peace, passion, and joy wrapped up in a cute little package—huh!.....and more like *huh*—maybe I didn't really have all the peace and joy and satisfaction I thought I did....*huh*!

Terri spoke about knowing and working out God's plan for my life. Wait! I thought I had a plan—work hard for my employer, overachieve with tithes and offering, be good to those around me. It may have been a little bit boring, but it was a solid, sustainable plan.

But then God!

He came in to rescue me as I saw such a contrast from my good, satisfying life to what Terri was describing and demonstrating—a life of peace, passion, and bubbling-over joy. I began to examine my life. God used this half-pint sized little woman to jerk me up to the reality that through Him I can do anything! But hold on a second—I didn't even know what I wanted. I only knew what my employer wanted. Now what?

Terri explained that all I had to do was ask the Lord for direction. I'd heard that message all my life and used it to help me at work, but this time God used it to wake me up to the fact that He had (has always had) a dream for me. *Wow*! Well how was I going to know what that was?

When I got home, I did as Terri explained—or more to the point, as God explains in the Bible. I sought God on this issue; with an open heart and mind I told Him what He already knew, but it broke down the wall I'd constructed that allowed Him only so far into my life. I asked Him to shape the direction of my life and told Him I was scared because I didn't know where this would go, which made me uncomfortable because I had always been the one with the plan and solution.

It was only a matter of three days and the Lord poured out a plan to me—and so I applied my learning from Terri and just started taking notes of everything that came up inside of me as I engaged with God on this matter. There was this awesome weaving of my past experiences with things I'd told God I wanted, things I promised God, and His incredible things I hadn't ever expected! *Wow* again! I absolutely don't know how these things will be accomplished—as they can clearly only be accomplished through Him, but I am on that path now and have zero doubt that He will bring them to pass with my cooperation.

I have a new zeal in life. I still work diligently for my employer, but I don't dedicate my every waking and dreaming hour to work. I work a normal 40 to 50 hours a week and God continues to bless my work. But now I have a dream that I lean in on and it causes me to better prioritize my time and effort to living with a higher purpose, which can only be achieved through my God who loves me so much He rescued me from stable and boring to live with a greater influence and joy. My hope is in God—in previously unimagined ways! Glory be to my God, my Savior, my Lord. Amen!

One final thought and question for you: Are you rescued—living life from the mountain top with zeal and a fullness in your spirit to a point where you often can't wipe the grin off your face? If not, talk to your Heavenly Father—you won't believe what He has in store for you! I am already excited for you.

Lori Mahowald
Follower of Jesus Christ, my savior and Lord
United States

My 21-Year Overnight Success Story

PAUL S. ROGERS

Don't Die with the Music still inside you.
Dr Wayne Dyer

What do a successful commercial lawyer, a kite-surf instructor, a teacher and life coach have in common? Sounds like the beginning of a bad joke, right?

It is actually the story of my 21-year overnight success. The reason for telling my story is to inspire and delight you and leave you in a better place than where I found you.

Let's start at the beginning: the year Prince had his monster hit *1999*. I had just qualified as a commercial lawyer in the UK—t he culmination of seven years of hard graft through the rite of passage of education and training.

My commercial law career would span more than 10 years. I went from a person who was terrified of the phone and not having immediate answers for potential clients, to having my ear glued to the phone. I made partner in an astoundingly short time, going from one of the team to leading the team. I always worried I wouldn't be taken seriously as I was still young—and looked it. I achieved financial success in my late 20's and early 30's. At the time, I thought I was super cool—fast cars and even faster women.

However, I soon came to realize there was something missing, an itch I couldn't scratch, a yearning that could not be fulfilled with the latest gadget, car, or relationship. It was safe to say I wasn't the most likable person. It is when you start to realize this that you really see the extent of the landscape you have built over the years.

I had done what society had taught me: got an education, worked hard, got a good job and been successful. If this was success, I knew this wasn't me. I had followed my head and its best thinking had got me to this point and it had done its job. Well done. But I knew there was something more. I couldn't picture myself doing this for the rest of my days. I couldn't even remember when I had last taken a vacation.

The crack appeared in the shape of kite-surfing. I found this sport near where I lived. I trained and wasn't all that good, but I loved every sea salt-soaked minute of it. It spoke to a different part of me. Little did I know this would be the beginning of the end of me listening to my head and instead thinking with and listening to my heart.

Life handed out a lesson in adversity in the form of a commercial lead recession in 2008-2009. My market and prized contacts suddenly fell apart. This was my chance to make my move. I planned my escape and told my business associates I would be leaving law to become a kite surfing instructor. Imagine the reactions. Yes, you imagined correctly! I gave back the keys to my sports cars to the dealerships, rented my house and prepared for a 10-week intensive kite surfing training in the Dominican Republic. I figured the worst that could happen would be I'd have 10 weeks out of the office having fun.

I arrived, 35 years old, in 2009, in the land of beautiful tanned gods and goddesses, most of whom were on their gap year! They talked about one day getting a job. I talked about one day not having a job. I bumbled my way through the training but scored well in the exams. I was all set for a return to the UK to practice my new craft.

Back home, I spent a lot of time in a small kite school learning the ropes, helping out where I could. At the end of the season, the owner of the kite school told me he was done teaching and would be closing the school. I purchased the school and set about building a great kite school brand. Within three years, I owned and operated two kite schools: one in the UK and one in the Cayman

Islands. This really was living the dream! I had successfully escaped corporate life and had my own unique brand. However, like any good Hollywood blockbuster, the story's hero was set for a fall. This duly happened when my business associate saw things a different way—a way without me. In the Cayman Islands, when you lose your job, you also lose your residency. I had ten days to leave the island!

It was Christmas 2012, and like in the original story, there was indeed no room at the inn. My soon-to-be wife and I managed to find the summer house of one of her relatives to bunk down in, in snowy Quebec, Canada. We had no money, no job, no place of our own, and moved from 40 degree weather to – 30 in a few days. Fun times!

We had not given up the passion of wanting to serve others and soon had a new job as joint partners for a lovely guest house in southern Vermont. We researched the complicated US work permits procedure. The suggestion was that, to avoid uncertainty, the interviews for the work permits could be done at US embassies. We dutifully obtained our passport stamped work visas. We loaded our few belongings into a U-Haul truck and set off to the American border.

The border guard questioned why we had the work visa in our passports, as it was the border that had discretion in awarding work visas. We then went through an hour or so interview, where our qualifications were resoundingly rejected. He explained that he was not interested in what some embassy had to say. He decided we would not be coming to the USA. In shock, and from the nearest place that had a signal, a McDonald's, we had to tell our new employers we would not be able to come. They were as disappointed as we were.

We returned to my mother-in-law's home, dejected, and now penniless. As my wife is French Canadian, we decided we would establish ourselves in Quebec. Because I was only starting my immigration procedure, I was unable to work on my tourist visa until I had received my permanent residency. We looked for jobs that would pay enough for both of us to survive.

My wife found a job as a teacher on a Cree Indian reserve in the far north of Quebec. We were destined to spend five years with our Indian brothers and sisters—a very different experience! In January it was colder than forty below for most the month. The village operated entirely on its hunting seasons. In fall and spring we had moose break and goose break. All administrative organizations closed down as staff and students alike headed out for a week of hunting. Wolves occasionally visited and roamed the village after dark.

Life then took two shocking turns.

The first was that, shortly after being turned away by the border agents, I had noticed a lump on my back. I had it checked and was told if it changed, to let the doctors know. Nothing happened for nearly a year…and then it did change.

I got the call no one wants to hear. "I'm so sorry. It's malignant; you have cancer." The world went to hell in a hand basket. I don't really remember what happened next, but before I knew it, I was on a plane back to the UK to be with my parents and to start my treatments. The plan was put in place and I was to present myself at numerous appointments. The weird thing was that I felt fine and a bit of a fraud, as hospitals are for sick people.

I needn't have concerned myself; three surgeries and testing made me ill enough to be there. After my last operation—a large ancillary clearance, as the little alien had managed to make it into the lymph nodes in my armpit—it was gone. To this day, it has stayed gone.

At this stage you would be forgiven for taking a break from the story to process all of what I have set out before you. As they say, the best is yet to come. Life delivered its second shocking turn with great magnitude.

On 19 March 2018, my life as I knew it ended. In the blink of an eye, it was all gone. My family and I were in a car, having just picked up my little 2 year-old boy from daycare. As we drove over an unmanned rail crossing in North Quebec, our car was hit by a train! Our son, amazingly, was fine, but my wife and I spent the next 10 days on life support. Our chances of pulling through were slim. My wife woke up a day before me and asked the nurses if she could come and see me. Not that she remembers this. The next day I woke up.

My poor parents had been informed of the accident and were told they needed to get out to northern Canada as fast as they could, as they might have make the decision to turn things off. When they arrived, the doctors raced to greet them, saying, "Forget what we said! He's awake!" It was nothing to do with them or their care, they told my parents. It was a miracle.

'Miracle' is such an easy and common word used in society. But when doctors and nurses from the intensive care unit use it, it means something.

My son's survival was another miracle. At the time of the accident, my beautiful white husky malamute, Sikou, was in in the car behind the rear seats. The firefighters said when they arrived at the car, my dog had, on the moment of impact, jumped over the rear seats on top of my wife and son. They would not have survived if he had not done so. He sadly did not make it but his final act was one of pure love to save his family.

I share this small side story to show that even in the midst of a completely destructive act, when the darkness is at its greatest, there is always a story of hope if you look for it. It is like finding a flower in a bomb crater. I have immortalized him in my books *The White Wolf's Way* (pen name Kate Summers).

The long journey of recovery started, but the injuries were horrific—broken neck, broken back, smashed skull, just to give a few highlights. The journey continues to this day, with each day stained with pain as well as the resulting psychological injuries.

Would I change what happened if I had the chance to go back? No, not a single thing.

Why? I have found my true life purpose and passion. It is to help others who are struggling with trauma find their purpose and passion. I have found true spirituality; a bang on the head tends to help with this. I have been given another roll of life's dice and this time it is going to count. I live with a pay-it-forward and gratitude mindset. My goal is to reach millions of people all over the planet to make an impact in their lives, so that they can to pay it forward, too.

Do you want to know my secret? How I've gotten through all of this without becoming bitter or a victim? I will tell you. You have an untapped inner strength that resides in you. You have faced your own challenges. What you may not have realized is that each challenge brings with it a gift. If you're like me, you never knew. If you now look behind, you will see a mountain of gifts you have given yourself and never unwrapped. In those gifts, you will find all you ever needed: strength, courage, passion, and much more. The secret is that you have everything you ever need inside you.

I thank you for reading my story. I also thank you in advance for being one of the people I have reached. At the beginning of my story, I held the hope that I would inspire you and leave you in a better place than when I found you. I hope I have done that. Whatever your challenge, or events you're facing, use my story as your survival guide. A map of inspiration and strength to overcome your trauma. You are never alone; I am with you in your fight. I salute you, my fellow sister and brother warriors.

Paul S. Rogers
Transformational expert, Thought leader, podcast host, speaker & coach and knowledge broker
United States

Abandonment to Joy

MEGAN KLINE

I could say that I have had a rough life so far, but that would be an understatement. My life prior to encountering God was full of abuse, abandonment, poor decisions, bad relationships, and lots of hate and anger. Deep down though, I always felt there was something or someone reaching for me. After having been through so much, I can now look back and know that God was there with me every step of the way. In every moment, God was watching over me, prompting me and leading me. I may not have listened all the time, or even most of the time, but He was there.

My life started as any other. My mother and father were married and had two daughters: myself and my older sister. I do not remember any fighting between my parents or any other major problems, but once I was older my mom explained to me what had happened. My father had started using drugs and left her for another woman. Not long after he left, he decided he did not want to pay child support or have anything to do with my sister and I, so he signed his parental rights away. This was my first taste of feeling abandoned and unloved.

I was four.

My mom also told me later that when I found out he had left, I told her he was dead. When I think back on what I must have felt, it makes me ache. I was Daddy's little girl. How could he not love me anymore? What could be more important? Was I not good enough? Those lies took hold in my heart, and that was when I first started feeling unworthy of love. It was my first case of a broken heart, the first time my world was shattered.

My mother remarried, and I remember thinking that I would have a dad again. Not long after this though, the sexual abuse started. I was five years old. I remember feeling so much shame and anger toward myself. I was disgusted with myself. I questioned what was wrong with me; what had I done to deserve it? My whole sense of the right and wrong ways to be loved was turned upside down and I began to think that the only way to gain someone's love was to do whatever they asked.

After years of being told I would get into trouble if I said anything about it, I finally worked up the courage to tell my mother. I remember sitting on her bed with her; she was holding a shotgun and we were waiting for my stepdad to come home. She confronted him and he did not deny it.

Nothing changed.

This was the second time I felt the pain of abandonment. On top of this, imagine also the feelings of not being heard, protected, and loved. I realized I was alone; no one was going to be there for me except me. I was devastated, to say the least. I was taught to not talk about what was happening to me, but to push it down and not acknowledge my feelings. So, I locked everything inside and the hatred grew. My questions became: why did my mom not love me? Was I not important to her? Did I not matter? I wondered if every child's life was this way or if I was the exception because I had done something wrong. It was the second time my heart was broken. My world shattered again.

I was nine.

Life went on with me pretending I was fine, but all the while I was hiding behind a mask. At one point, I remember my mom taking me to counseling. Throughout the whole session, I did not talk. My mom was furious and asked me why I would not talk. I told her it was because I had nothing to say. I remember thinking: *Why would I talk about my feelings and things that have happened when I have been told not to? I have been warned that bad things could happen if I told.*

I started smoking cigarettes and marijuana at the age of thirteen. At that time, I mostly did it because my friends were doing it. I did not tell anyone about the abuse I had suffered until I was fifteen. The first time I did so, I mentioned it nonchalantly to a friend and I immediately regretted it. My friend told our school guidance counselor, and I was called to the guidance office. I remember being extremely nervous and anxious. I went in and Child Protection Services was with the counselor. I was questioned, but I denied everything. I lied, just as I had been taught to.

After school, I went home and was bombarded with questions about what I had said. I assured my mother I had not told the truth and had denied all the accusations. She told me that was good because I knew what could happen if I told. Again, I felt like an inconvenience; I felt unloved and unwanted. I felt like I was hated and so my shame grew. I did not have anyone I could trust or anywhere I could go. No one would believe me, and no one would help me. I did not understand what I had done wrong or why I had to go through all this turmoil.

Every month, I went to an all-night skate at the skating rink in the neighboring town. It happened to be the night of my encounter with Child Protection that I went, even though my head was reeling, and my heart was breaking even more, filling up with anger and hate. Looking back, I have realized that if I had not gone skating that night, I would have committed suicide. I felt that alone.

While I was at the all-nighter, I met a man. He was twenty years old and he showed an interest in me, so I left the all-nighter to smoke marijuana with him and a few other people. I soon found out he was wanted for robbery and so he was about to flee to Florida with a friend. I told them I wanted to go with them, and it was agreed between us. We took the other people back to the skating rink, and after being asked a thousand times if I was sure about it, I left for Florida with them.

We were there for two weeks before we were pulled over, closely followed by us fleeing from the cops in a high-speed chase, which culminated in us wrecking the car. We were all handcuffed and taken to jail. The guys were placed in cells and I was put in the office, where the officer repeatedly asked my name, hometown, and age. I was reluctant to give these details, as I was not sure I wanted to go home. However, he eventually figured out my identity and called my mother, explaining to her what had happened.

The officer took me to a runaway shelter until my mom could come and pick me up. The people there asked why I had run away, but I still refused to talk about it. A day or two later, my mom came. I told her I would not return home unless things changed, and she promised me they would. I found out later that when I disappeared, my mom thought my stepfather had killed me.

Upon returning home, I found out lots of people had been looking for me. My biological father even came to see me (I had only seen him a few times since he left). He wanted to be part of my life again. I was unsure as to whether I could trust him, but I wanted to try. At this stage, my mother and stepfather divorced, so I did not see my stepfather much anymore.

My relationship with my mother worsened however, and I felt I was on the receiving end of even more hatred and dislike, as she blamed me for her divorce. I became rebellious and started spending time with the wrong people. I began drinking, using more drugs, and smoking cigarettes heavily. I was suicidal and extremely depressed by this stage. I felt even more unloved and unwanted than before; I was so completely alone. I began cutting myself to deal with the pain.

At the age of sixteen, I drank so much that I gave myself alcohol poisoning. At the time, I was staying in Ohio with a relative, and we had decided to drink together. I drank until all my pain and bad memories seemed to go away. The next thing I remember is waking up in the hospital with an IV in my arm to the sight of people standing over me. I sat up and tried to leave. The doctors told me if the police officer who picked me up and brought me to the hospital had been just a few minutes later, I would not have made it. They informed me they had pumped my stomach three or four times and that I had consumed enough alcohol to kill two grown men—I was sixteen and weighed around ninety pounds.

This was the scare I needed to stop drinking and doing drugs. I found new friends and started working at a fast-food restaurant, where I met my first husband.

We started dating when I was sixteen. He was four years older than me. About that time, I had been driving without a license one night and caused a major car accident. My mother grounded me and told me I was no longer allowed to see or speak to my boyfriend. The next day she caught me on the phone with him and gave me an ultimatum. I could either stop seeing and talking to him or I could marry him.

I called her bluff and said I would marry him, and she signed off on the marriage a few months later. Not long into the marriage however, my new husband became abusive. This abuse was physical, mental, and emotional. He controlled everything I did. I could not go to school or work or visit family and friends. Worse yet, a few months into our marriage, he murdered a woman who lived three doors down from our apartment.

I remember one morning, when it was still incredibly early, I woke up to the sound of him in the shower. I knew this was extremely odd, but I was groggy and hardly awake because he had me take sleeping pills every night before bed. The next thing I remember is him waking me and telling me he was going to his mother's house. I was confused, but still groggy, and he would not explain why he was leaving. He said no more than that he needed to go for a few days. I knew better than to argue or question further, so I just went back to sleep.

The next time I woke up, it was to the sound of our telephone ringing. I knew it was him and it made me nervous. When I saw police cars, fire trucks, and an ambulance in our complex's parking lot, I became scared. I answered the phone and told him what I saw outside, but he did not want me to get off the phone. I hung up on him and went to investigate. I knew I would get in a lot of trouble, but I needed to know what was happening. I opened our front door with my stomach tying itself in knots. Why was I so nervous and anxious? The smell hit me first.

It was an awful smell mixed with smoke—it was the smell of burnt flesh, but I didn't know that yet. The noise was the next thing to hit me and I was stuck there in my open front door, afraid to move, just watching. I finally decided I needed to move and find out what had happened, so I went to a neighbor's house and asked them. They told me there was a fire and they thought someone had been injured, but they didn't know for sure.

At that point, the manager of the complex knocked on their door asking to use a phone. These neighbors didn't have one so I offered mine. We walked to my apartment and I let her in. Half-listening to her conversation, I overheard there was a dead woman and the police were investigating it as a possible homicide. My heart sank and my fear grew. After the manager left, I went back to the neighbors and told them what I had heard.

Finally, I decided to go home and clean myself up. When I flipped the light on in our bathroom, I noticed a red streak on the light switch cover.

I knew it was blood.

I knew it was from my husband.

I felt sick to my stomach. I could feel in my gut that something was wrong, but I pushed it down and refused to listen to my instincts.

In the evening, my husband called, and I begged him to come home. I was so scared and completely alone. They had no idea who could be responsible for the homicide and I did not want to be alone while this was going on, but he refused to come home. The blood on the light switch and the fact that he was not willing to come home made my stomach hurt. I knew deep down in my heart that he had something to do with the murder.

He came home a couple of days later, and I was furious with him. I yelled and screamed at him for leaving me alone. He kept telling me it was fine; that he had known nothing would happen. After arguing for a while, I became very calm and quietly said, "It was you, wasn't it?"

He stared at me for what seemed an eternity. I asked again. He started to speak and then stopped. I stared at him, knowing what he was going to say.

"Yes, it was me," he finally said.

"You need to tell me everything. I have to know," I immediately told him. I'm not sure if I was more stunned by this than he was, but I felt something telling me I needed to know every little detail. He told me just about everything (except for one detail I found out later). When I asked him why he killed her, he told me it was because she would not fight back. I asked why he had not killed me, to which he replied it was because I always fought back. Somehow, I remained calm throughout the entire conversation. After my questions were answered, he told me if I told anyone, anyone at all, or if I left him, he would kill my sister, her two little boys, my mother, and my brother.

Not long after this, my biological father fell ill. He had been diagnosed with throat cancer some months before but was in remission. This time, he had been diagnosed with brain cancer and was given only a month or two to live. I spent as much time with him as possible. I had had barely two years with him, and it devastated me that I was losing him again. I felt so helpless and hopeless. I wanted so badly for him to get better, but he did not. He took his last breath as I sat next to him. Just before he died, he had a pastor come to his home. As a result, my father was saved. He told me I needed to be saved, too, but I had no idea then what that meant.

For nine long, agonizing months, I had to stay and play the perfect little wife—who got beaten up if she stepped out of line. I called my mother once, but she had refused to come and get me, instructing me to call my dad, although I no longer had a father. Toward the end of the eighth month, my mom asked me if I would go on a trip with her to Texas for two weeks over the course of the next month.

I knew my husband would never let me go, but not long after this I read an article in the newspaper revealing that the murdered woman had been raped after she was dead. This revelation pushed me over the edge. I told my husband I would be leaving with my mom and if he refused to let me, I would disappear forever. Only God knows why, but he said I could go.

We left and we were gone for two weeks. The night before our return, my husband called me and said, "They picked me up."

I did not understand what this meant at first but then he explained they had picked him up for the murder. I felt such relief, as if I could breathe again! I sobbed so much on the phone, and he kept telling me everything would be fine. But I was not crying for his sake; I was crying for mine, because I was finally free.

My mother and I left in the morning to come home. When she asked me if she needed to take me home or if my husband would be picking me up, I told her he would not be able to pick me up for a long time. She looked at me strangely and asked what I meant, so I told her everything. She had to pull over to gain her composure. For the remainder of the journey, she kept telling me what she thought I needed to do and that I needed to go to the police right away, but I insisted I would handle things in my own way. I knew I had to make sure he was really in jail.

I made trips to my brother-in-law's house and to the jail, to ensure my husband was really there and would be staying there. Then I had a family friend accompany me back to the jail so I could talk to the detective in charge of the case. They called the detective in, and it seemed to take an eternity for him to arrive. I was taken into a room where I told them everything I knew, based on everything my husband had told me, every single detail. They recorded everything I said. A few months later, I was asked to have a recorded conversation with my husband that verified the details I had told them.

After the trial, the detective told me that had I not come forward, my husband would have gotten away with murder and would most likely have become a serial killer, as he had already started stalking other victims. I, however, felt only the guilt of not having come forward sooner, for how that might have affected the woman's family, and the thought that maybe, if he had killed me instead, she would not have had to die. However, I know now that I did not have control over my husband's actions, and that I did the best I could with what I had to work with. I kept others from being harmed as best I could—at least the ones I know of.

By the time I was nineteen, we were divorced. I went back to school and got my high school diploma, doing my junior and senior years in one year. I progressed through life as best I could, never really trusting or giving my heart fully to anyone. I continuously sabotaged anything and everything that was good in my life. I did not feel I deserved to be loved or happy. I pretended well that I was fine, that everything was good; but the turmoil inside me can only be described as a tornado of emotion. It entailed hate and anguish over everything I had been through, even hatred towards myself. I had completely stopped loving myself. I did not so much as like who I was, so I was unable to genuinely love others. Every day, I hid behind the same mask I had put on when I was a little girl, a brave face to keep the world from seeing the pain inside.

I was twenty-two when I began dating a guy I had known since I was nine years old. He was into drugs and I made the choice to start using them, too. I had lost everything following a break-up with a guy I dated soon after leaving my ex-husband. I was losing control completely. I did not know where to turn and I always felt alone and unloved. For two years, I was in the clutches of methamphetamines, until one day I woke up to an audible thought racing through my mind saying, "This is not the life for you."

That day, I decided I was done using drugs and wanted to get clean. It did not happen overnight, but each day my willpower grew stronger. I did not go to rehab or have any help; I just did it. A few months later, I found out I was pregnant. I thank God every day for giving me the willpower to stop using drugs. When I think about what could have happened had I not chosen to listen to my intuition, it makes me cringe. My son was three when we left his father. I had lost control of myself again and was tail spinning through life.

At twenty-eight, then, I found myself the mother of a three-year-old, pregnant again, and married to a man I should not be married to. We had been married a week or two when I took that pregnancy test. I knew without a doubt that he was not the father, as we had only been together between three and four weeks. You read that right: I married a man I had known for only two weeks.

I knew who the father was, and he was married to

someone else. We had not spoken to each other in over a month. I was not prepared to be pregnant, nor did I want to be. I was jobless, pretty much homeless, and in a bad marriage.

My husband was becoming abusive but seeing as I had vowed after my first marriage that I would not stay in another abusive relationship, we separated. I went back to live with my mom but a few weeks later, I returned to the father of my three-year-old, as we had decided to get back together. He told me he would stand by me no matter what my decision was regarding the baby, but I knew things were not just magically going to improve with him.

On the one hand, I could choose abortion. I thought and thought about it. I did not know God at this stage, was not a Christian, and I had never been a regular church attendee. I had prayed before, but not to a personally known God. So, here I was, twenty-eight years old, pregnant, and considering abortion. It was something others had suggested. I did some research and for one fleeting moment really considered it. My conscience, however, stopped me. I know now that it was God prompting me. I did not really believe in abortion and I knew myself well enough to at least know I could not go through with it.

I tried to wrap my head around the idea of keeping the baby, but the more I thought about it, the more I knew my unborn baby and my son deserved more out of life than I could give to them. It was not that I did not have enough love for both; it was that I knew their lives would be so much harder if I raised them both. I was already raising my son by myself, while working full-time, and our situation with his father was not good. Our relationship was not healthy, and neither were some of the other things he was doing. The baby's father was not in the picture.

So, I prayed. This was the first time I ever prayed and truly meant it, the first time I ever called out to a God I did not know, wanting Him to respond. Our God is so faithful to all of us, even those who do not know Him yet. This is where my faith journey began. This is where healing from my past hurts and abuses began.

Please understand that it did not just happen all at once, but that the seed was planted at this stage. I was extremely depressed and anxious about everything. I had to mentally separate myself from the baby growing in my womb so I could make it through the heart-wrenching pain of knowing I could not take care of this baby.

I was prompted to consider adoption. I researched it, looking up lawyers that dealt with adoption, and adoption agencies. I prayed, and I prayed, and I prayed. Finally, I chose. I chose adoption. I chose to do the hardest thing I have ever had to do, the hardest thing I have ever been through. It was harder than all the abuse, overcoming addiction, or any other major event I have gone through in my life. I contacted a lawyer's office that dealt specifically with adoptions. They were located a few hours away, but they were willing to come to me for a meeting.

I did not stop praying just because I had made my decision. I continued to pray and continued to ask God to give me strength. I continued to ask God for a family that would love the precious child growing inside me. I met with the lawyer and I also took more time to think and pray. I started looking through profiles of potential adoptive parents. I kept praying for God to show me a specific couple, the right couple. I looked through hundreds of profiles, but I kept coming back to one in particular—I could not explain why. I would look at their profile and then at four or five others, but my attention was always drawn right back to theirs. I asked the lawyer to see if they would be interested in meeting.

We met a week or two later at a coffee shop close to where I lived. I was so nervous and scared. So many what-ifs were running through my head. I did not want to speak or move, let alone breathe. We talked and we all asked and answered each other's questions. I had some specific requests for them regarding doctor appointments and the delivery. We talked more until the meeting was over. I told them I would let the lawyer know my decision, and I went home. It did not take me long to let the lawyer know I would like to place my baby with this couple.

They were wonderful and were everything I had hoped they would be.

The pregnancy went by smoothly and the couple reliably attended every appointment. The delivery went well, and the adoptive mother was allowed in to have the baby once he was born, via a planned C-section. I received updates every three months for the first year, and following that, I received them once a year until the child reached the age of five. We decided to continue updates beyond the five-year mark. He is so loved.

When I came home from the hospital without my baby, I sank deeper into depression. I was so alone, and I hated myself even more. I would tell myself I was stupid and deserved to feel this pain, that I did not deserve love or happiness. I was extremely hard on myself. I felt like a failure. I did not want to go on, but I had a little boy who looked to me, who loved me and wanted me. So, I put my mask on again and tucked all my feelings deep down inside.

I know now that it was not my own strength that carried me through that pregnancy, delivery, hospital stay, and all the time after: It was God. Even though I had yet to know Him personally, God orchestrated such a perfect and divine plan. I thank Him every day.

I look back on my whole life and I can see all the things God has done to protect and save me. There were so many times He could have just thrown up his hands and said, "I'm done!" but He never did.

These are two of my favorite verses:

Isaiah 43:18-19 (NIV) "Forget the former things; do not dwell on the past. See, I am doing a new thing! Now it springs up; do you not perceive it? I am making a way in the wilderness and streams in the wasteland."

Jeremiah 29:11 (NIV) "For I know the plans I have for you," declares the LORD, "plans to prosper you and not to harm you, plans to give you hope and a future.

Megan Kline
Stay-home mama!
Associates Degree in Business Management
Associates Degree in Biblical Studies and Ministry
United States

It Took My Death to Learn How to Live

ALANNA MARTELLA

To most people, September 8, 2008 is just another day in the past; a day that came and went like the waves in the sea—here for a moment, before flitting away in the blink of an eye; a day that most people probably can't remember the specifics of. But not for me.

You see, September 8th, 2008, is the day I died. Not died in a metaphorical sense, but in a literal sense: heart stopped, no pulse, flat-lined. I literally died.

Spoiler alert! The doctors and nurses were able to save me, but what followed was a long, painful recovery on every level: physical, mental, emotional, and spiritual.

Despite all of the pain and the mental anguish, I wouldn't trade my experience for the world. In fact, September 8th, 2008, was the best day of my life. It granted me a second chance — the opportunity to make things right. And let me tell you, I was most certainly not doing things "right" before this.

I was a senior in high school, hell-bent on getting

straight As and being the absolute best runner there was. I was so obsessed with running that I woke up at 4 a.m. before school to run for miles. I skipped family vacations —such as my parents' weekly trips to our lake house at Dale Hollow Lake in Tennessee or my cousin's graduation from law school on the East Coast. I skipped social activities with my high school friends because I feared these things would get in the way of my running.

And what kind of life is that? It's not a life at all!

I knew changes had to be made, but I couldn't wrap my mind around how to make those changes. I wasn't as mentally strong then as I am now. Little did I know that the change I needed would come in the form of a medical catastrophe that entailed countless nights in hospital, over a dozen surgeries, modifications to my diet, and more.

Let me walk you through the day it all began: September 8th, 2008.

It was like any other day. I woke up at 4 a.m. for my crazy girl run before school, went to school, ran again, and then visited my grandma at her nursing home with my dad.

While I was at my grandma's, I started to feel a pain in my abdomen. The pain was so intense it felt as if my insides were on fire. Even curling on the floor in the fetal position didn't provide respite.

I thought maybe I was hungry, so when we left, we

went to Panera Bread to see if eating some food could help ease the pain.

Once we got to Panera, I made a beeline to the bathroom thinking that has *got* to be why I am in so much pain! But as I reached the bathroom, I fell to the floor in pain. I remember pressing my hot face against the cool tile floor and not wanting to move because the cold surface felt so good on my burning-up body. I stayed there so long that my dad came into the bathroom and found me lying there.

The pain continued for hours until I lay in my bed that night, seeing the big, bright moon and thinking, because there was nothing that could fix the pain: *Please let me die right now.* This pain was so intense that I wouldn't wish the world's most evil tyrants to feel this pain, truly.

I got up again to go to the bathroom in the middle of the night and I passed out. My dad heard me hit the vanity in the bathroom with a smack and found me on the floor. He felt for my pulse, which he counted as a racing 167 beats per minute—significantly higher than the average resting heart rate of 60 and 100.

He knew I was in trouble and called 911. An ambulance came and rushed me to the hospital. I remember the ride to the emergency room, feeling so much pain and anguish. I went to hold the hand of one of the EMT's in the back of the ambulance but he pulled his hand away. I don't know why this sticks out in my memory, but it does. I remember thinking it was very cruel at the time. Later though, I learned from one of my EMT friends that medical technicians often try to put up a guard to prevent themselves being affected by the sights they see on a daily basis, just in case something were to happen to one of their patients. It helps them maintain emotional distance. I guess I can understand this mentality now, to an extent.

But I digress.

In the ER, I still needed the bathroom. I was also confused because my mom was there as well. I asked her to help me to the bathroom because I was in so much pain and was so lethargic that I couldn't walk myself.

She helped me into the bathroom and was holding me up. She says that all of a sudden, I went limp. At that moment, a nurse walked in with a urine cup saying, "We need a urine sample!" to which my mom replied, "I think she's dead!"

The nurse took one look at me, according to my mom, and called a double code. Dozens of healthcare workers rushed to my aid and my mom kept repeating "Is she dead? Is she dead?" and someone answered, "She's not responding," as they rushed me away on a stretcher.

As doctors and nurses were racing to save my life, I was on a separate journey. It was a journey to the other side that most people don't make it back from to share with the world.

This journey was unlike any I've ever experienced. I was walking down the beach with a figure dressed in a shrouded white gown next to me. I'd like to think it was Jesus. We were walking along this beach toward a light that kept getting brighter and brighter as we continued, but it was not a brightness that hurts the eyes.

I remember feeling so at peace during this walk, so at ease with myself that it felt as if I were floating. We continued this silent, tranquil walk and at the end of the beach, there was a gateway. I looked beyond the gate to see my Great Aunt Fedora, who I called DoDo. She had been my favorite person in the world, and she had passed when I was a toddler. I was the one who discovered she was dead, but that's another story.

She had her arms outstretched and said, "Come to me, baby." I remember wanting to go to her so badly! I took a look at the gateway and began to push open the door. I started to take a step in when the figure next to me said, "Stop. It's not your time."

Then, I woke up. I woke up in the emergency room with healthcare workers surrounding me. I saw my parents crying at the back of the room. I looked to my right and asked the doctor next to me if I was going to be okay, to which he responded, "We're going to do the best we can."

It was in that moment I knew I was in trouble.

It's so true that your life flashes before your eyes when you're nearing your last moments. It isn't just a Hollywood thing. I immediately thought of all the could-haves and should-haves and all the things I wish I would have said but never did. I thought of my mom and how I couldn't die on her—I was her only child! I thought of how I'd never gone skydiving like I always said I wanted to do. I thought of how I'd never walk down the aisle and get married.

And it was in this moment, as I was thinking of all this, that I made a vow to myself to pull through and make sure I never returned to the life of mediocrity and repetition I had been living.

I truly believe this journey to the other side remains the pivot point in my life, the transitional moment in which I went from being an obsessive teenage girl to a free-spirited young woman.

The doctors wheeled me back for emergency surgery. It turned out my intestines had been twisting. I had died from sepsis, brought about by the strangulation, and my intestines were so dead they crumbled in the doctor's hands. I had 15 feet of my small intestines removed.

I had to get an ostomy bag for a few months while my remaining intestines healed (though they originally thought I might need it for life) and I had to receive IV nutrition via a port which was implanted in my chest because I couldn't eat or drink anything.

The ostomy bag was *extremely* humiliating. It would sometimes break without a moment's notice, spilling its contents all over my body. Imagine that smell!

However, I was determined to reverse the need for a ostomy bag and be able to live a "normal" life. My mom and I would pray to God each night before I went to bed and envision my intestines healing and me being able to live bag-free.

A couple of months later, I had a procedure that showed that my intestines had healed, meaning I could get my ostomy bag take-down!

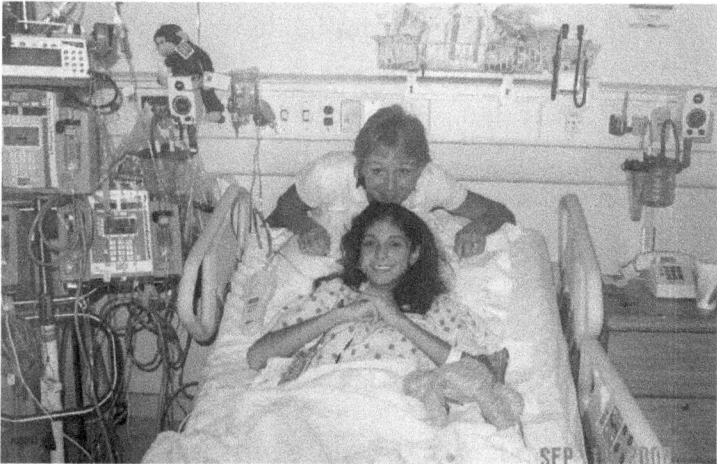

I believe whole-heartedly that the power of prayer is what allowed this healing to happen.

Fast forward a little over a decade later, and here I

am, living (for the most part) normally. I still have ups and downs and even had to have another surgery just a couple of months prior to writing this. But, I am alive—with no ostomy bag and maybe more importantly, with a whole new lens on life.

Let me lay out a blueprint of what this ordeal taught me about life, and maybe it'll give you something to take away and hold onto, without having to go through an ordeal like the one I experienced.

1. Understand the value of each minute, every second you are alive. Wake up each day excited to tackle whatever might be thrown at you, because who knows, it could be your last day! Every day before I jump out of bed I say: "Great day, great day, today is going to be a great day!" and by saying it and affirming it, the universe learns that I am going to have a great day and that I am a force to be reckoned with.

2. Follow your dreams and don't give up until they become a reality. And, if your dreams change, steer those sails and bring your next dream to life. And while steering those sails, *never* let anyone tell you you're a quitter. You simply learned that that which you initially dreamed is not your true dream or calling.

3. The best gifts you will ever receive are your relationships with others. Cherish the time spent with everyone, especially the people you love and care for. Make sure they feel that love and care.

I'll admit, remembering these "rules" isn't always easy, but each year as September 8th rolls around, I'm given a little refresher course on how far I have come and how much further I can go.

And you know what? I will.

And you know what? You will too.

Take it from me. Allowing yourself to embrace and enjoy this life you were gifted with will give you something to look back on and smile about, sans regrets, when it's your time to leave this earth.

Alanna Martella
Multi-Emmy Winning TV Broadcaster; Keynote Speaker;
Board Member for the Make-A-Wish Ohio, Kentucky &
Indiana Southern Ohio Region Branch;
RYT-200 (Registered Yoga Teacher)
United States

Instagram: @alannamartella
Twitter: @AlannaMartella
YouTube: Alanna Martella
Facebook: www.facebook.com/alannamartella

Overcoming
HQ

ERIK SCOTT

I grew up on Long Island New York, in the 1980's. My home life was filled with screaming and yelling, drunken slurring and the sounds of slamming doors, fists hitting, and cracking bones. My sister and I often hid in the hall closet or ran across the street as we waited for the police to show up and take my father out in handcuffs again. We thought this was normal.

My parents, both alcoholics, lived a life of partying, largely non-existent in our home. They divorced when I was young, resulting in my mother having to work three jobs just to keep our home. My sister and I mostly lived with our grandparents till I was 13.

What memories I have of my parents together are nothing short of traumatic: everything from seeing my father assaulting my mother, to watching my mother bring home new men every weekend. I remember my father chasing us out of the house one night with a running chainsaw, then pulling our car into the middle of the road and using it for target practice with his hunting bow. I was about 6 at the time.

Though my parents' marriage was a disaster, my grandparents were very traditional. Once I turned 13, I wanted nothing more than to get away from my home because I felt so disconnected from reality. I set goals for myself, one of which was to complete high school and get out of New York.

I fit in well in high school, and was friendly with nearly everyone. I played ice hockey, and my coach helped me through this time. I looked to him as a mentor and father figure. When he took me under his wing, I learned there were good men out there and not just alcoholics. I listened to what he said, especially when it came to the use of drugs and alcohol. And yet, this didn't stop me from slowly going down the path I so desperately wanted to stay away from.

My community was a high drug trafficking area, so getting drugs was easy. I stayed away from it because I didn't want to let my coach down. Nor did I want to turn out like my father. But life has a way of not following our plans.

I became homeless during my last year of high school. I was a 17-year-old kid living in my car while still attending high school. I took on this life challenge while working part time making $97.00 a week. It didn't matter. My mind was set. I was going to make it regardless! I wanted to start a business, and I did, launching my first business, MAD Solutions Detailing, in June of 1997—the same month I graduated high school and while I was still homeless. Things were going to get worse, however, rather than better.

In 1998 I dropped out of college. I was a young kid making good money. My life began to spiral out of control with a series of poor decisions, including falling into alcohol and drugs, which became a daily battle. In 2001 everything came crashing down.

My mother was diagnosed with cancer in July of that year, and in September, as I was crossing the Verrazano bridge, the truly unthinkable occurred. Gazing over the water, I watched the attack on the World Trade Center unfold. It was unfathomable; as a proud New Yorker, I was in shock. I quickly contacted and volunteered for the search and rescue efforts. That time will never be erased from my memory, nor will the smell ever be forgotten.

And yet—I continued my life of run-ins with the law, fights, and days and nights in and out of the hospital. By 2003, I knew I had to do something different or I was going to die, so I walked into a local military recruiting office and joined the U.S. Navy in June of 2004.

I arrived at boot camp with a chip on my shoulder, still rebelling against authority, but a few weeks in boot camp quickly cured that. I was now a proud Navy sailor, trusted and relied upon to help others. I felt great after having no alcohol or drugs for weeks! It was the first time I was really sober in nearly six years. But it wasn't long before I was once again jeopardizing my life—and my new career.

In late November of 2004, a few of my friends and I went drinking. We ended up at a local hotel and a fight broke out. I unfortunately do not remember much of what happened, but I do remember being detained by the local Norfolk police, and turned over to the command. Two weeks later, I was informed I would be charged with drunk and disorderly. I was completely embarrassed.

Fast forward thirteen years and we come to the turning point of my life. I had returned from a year long deployment to find myself facing a new way of life. I had just lost my mother, and my wife, Rebecca, and I had a new baby. Struggling to re-acclimate to family life, I felt heavy. I sought out the chaplin on a few occasions. The deployment I had just come off of was filled with special ops and joint task operations. Our missions were classified. You never really "saw" anything, from sending operators out and not receiving them back for days. You just knew.

I started to have a hard time seeing reality. I became distant from friends and family. I seemed normal enough at work, but at home I couldn't connect with my wife, I couldn't connect with my children, and for six months I had trouble sleeping. I was plagued with constant nightmares. Through it all, I was too prideful to think about seeking help.

Things improved somewhat and I continued to go to work with a smile on my face. At home, though, it was a different story. There was arguing and bickering, over taking out the trash or loading the dishwasher or any number of things. It was during this time we learned my wife was pregnant again with our fourth child.

My newest daughter arrived November 2, 2015, the day after our seventh wedding anniversary. I was distant. I didn't want to hold her, like I had the others. I was now pushing myself away from my family.

The tension at home was thick, the arguments became more frequent, and in January 2016, for the first time, my wife and I spoke the word *divorce* in a fight. It took me back to my childhood, to watching my family fall apart. Seeing the arguing and fighting led me to once again think, *I'm not good enough.* I felt worthless, and insecure about myself both as a person and a man. Looking back now, how hurt Rebecca had to have been to even bring up divorce.

While I faced my greatest personal challenges at home, work was functioning well above normal. I led my division and served in numerous other leadership capacities. I was firm, and fair with all my sailors, giving them what I saw to be the right guidance. I set nothing but the highest expectations for them to reach their professional and personal goals. It was my mission now to lead sailors but unlike any other traditional way of leadership.

And yet—as a leader in my home, I was a failure. My pride and ego continued getting in the way. I had complete trust from my command, but it was broken in my home. The numerous arguments we had through April and May of 2016 left me feeling that my family life and marriage were over.   In June of 2016, I looked my wife in the eye and told her I no longer loved her and was leaving her. Every day prior to leaving I told myself I never wanted to end up like my parents—a torn marriage, another broken home, and children who would be raised without a father.

I was dying inside and fighting daily battles within myself. I had stood strong on my professional values for so long but now I couldn't face the fact that my marriage and family were over. I started living in my truck, because I couldn't face my wife. I fought myself everyday to go home or make it permanent, but I had lost hope of being able to fix things.

I continued to work like any other day, but I started seeking attention from other women because this was the only way I felt complete. I descended further into feeling I was not good enough for my family, that I was a failure as a father.

I left my wife for several weeks, trying to find who I truly was.

Finally, on July 3, 2016, a Saturday, my wife and I decided to take the children to the Virginia Aquarium, for us to talk about our future.

It was here I was able to open up about all the pain I'd been feeling, the challenges of completing her as a husband, my insecurities about being a good husband and father, and all that had occurred while I'd been gone. We talked about relying on another person to share my problems with and trusting my feelings. Being open and honest about what had occurred over the past few weeks helped in re-laying the groundwork to slowly repair our marriage.

Shortly after I returning home in July 2016, I was scheduled to attend a school in Florida. Just before I drove out of my driveway on a September day, my wife handed me a book called *The Purpose Driven Life* by Rick Warren. Instead of focusing on that, I decided to make one more trip down the road of alcohol. When I arrived in Florida I hit the bottle hard and kept going for nearly three weeks straight. I functioned well in school, and at the end of each day worked my way to the bottom of a bottle. Then came the message to evacuate Florida due to a hurricane bearing down on the coast. I decided to head home to Virginia until I was called back and so another twelve-hour drive ensued.

It was what happened three days later that completely changed my life.

On October 9th, 2016, I was recalled to school. I started the drive late. As a result of all the people displaced by the hurricane, there were no available hotel rooms. Around 2 a.m., I finally stopped for the night at a rest stop near Jacksonville on I-95 in Florida. I woke a few hours later around 8:30 a.m. and it was then the most horrific event of my life happened.

As I got out of my truck and closed the door, a man appeared behind me with a knife. He plunged it into my back. I fell to the ground, screaming for God to save me just one more time. A woman hurried up, asking if I was okay. I climbed to my feet, dazed, shaking off the attack —and realized there was no one there. I was all alone.

Looking back now, I believe I was being shown how I was attacking myself. I was the one killing me, and God helped me by completely and radically saving me on that day, October 10, 2016. This day will be forever ingrained and remembered as the day I was saved by God to live my life.

When I returned home in November 2016, I took Rebecca in my arms and apologized again for all the bad things I had done. I told her I wanted to make it up to her. My amends began. I told her about my life-changing experience and how God appeared to save me. I started to attend church, and to rebuild the trust I had destroyed in our home—not just with Rebecca, but with my children, and even myself.

As I was able to finally make amends with those I'd hurt, I was also being filled in a way that has changed me into who I am today. I was born again so completely during this time, that today I stand in front of people I've known for years and am unrecognizable. I am a new man with a new life and new faith; one who has taken all his past experience as lessons and learned, through a trial, to seek help.

Since then, so much has changed in my life. From 2016-2018 I developed and established a leadership training program where we speak about servant leadership, ethical voice, motivation, and resiliency. In our pilot, we earned a 97% approval rating. Today, our program has impacted over 20,000 people both in and out of the military.

In 2018, I launched a program called OvercomeHQ, where we lead, inspire, and drive young leaders to become a better self, while mentoring them through personal trials and traumatic events.

I developed and launched a consulting organization, OvercomeHQ, to help young people find their path, in a way I was unable to when I was younger. For the last year I have put many hours, as a personal development coach, into helping young people face adversity and recover.

My personal mission is to lead, inspire, and drive people to become a better self through developing life skills that help build confident and motivated individuals. Since starting, I have shared my story at numerous local events that help in the growth and development of young men seeking to improve their lives. I was personally invited by the Newport News public schools to speak at numerous events and recently conducted three 45-minute workshops, leading the discussion for over 350 students.

Additionally we work with underprivileged youth, and people who struggle with drug and alcohol, because since my day of saving, I have been completely sober, and fully believe that God is the reason why.

This leads me to my last moment of grace. As of today, I am working on completing my Masters Degree in Divinity with a concentration in Chaplaincy to serve those who need it most, and to serve through faith. Who I was then is no longer who I am today. I was able to address issues from my past, as far back as to when I was a child. Coupled with professional help, we have been able to face those issues head on, changed by God.

Erik Scott

Founder, OvercomeHQ, military
United States

Lyric Faith

L.C. POWELL

I've always had a strong faith in God. I consider it a gift. As I grew up, we moved a lot due to my father's military career. While houses, schools, and landscape changed frequently, one constant was the boxed set of *Lives of the Saints*, with beautiful gold covers —a set I still have today. At a very young age, I was entranced by the shiny, thick pages and full-color pictures that told the lives of these remarkable men and women of faith. I wanted the same strong faith they did.

But faith is rarely, if ever, built on an easy life. What need is there of faith when all is going smoothly? I've had plenty of opportunity for my faith to grow, but one of the earliest came with the end of high school and beginning of college. Our family always had issues. Family problems have deep roots, and it would take a whole book to delve into why we did. Suffice it to say, we did.

As we moved closer to my father's retirement and returned to my parents' hometown, our problems grew worse. My father suffered from back pain, which was just one cause of him drinking almost every night after dinner. He also had a quick temper.

My father was, at one point, diagnosed a 'dry drunk' – one who can quit drinking any time but will still display all the behaviors of an alcoholic. When I read the literature on alcoholic families, I felt the researchers had watched our family and told our story. Among the children in such families, there is always a scapegoat. That was invariably me.

It could be anything that raised my father's ire. One day, it was Pop Tarts. I had Pop Tarts, he accused, but didn't buy a birthday gift for my younger sister. When I told him my best friend had bought them and given them to me, it made no difference. He had set out to accuse me and facts were not going to sway him. I was in trouble for having Pop Tarts.

As I've grown older, and hopefully wiser, I've come to understand that often, a person's anger 'at' another is really their own internal frustrations with life, and seeking a place to vent that frustration. Such was the case in our home.

There was a night my junior year of high school that I came out of the shower in my parents' bathroom when my father had gone to bed early. The door slipped from my hand, slamming the chandelier into the mirror. It caused noise but no damage. My father flew into a rage, ranting and yelling at me. I held my tongue and didn't yell back, apologized, and left.

In retrospect, I believe he was upset about something else and spoiling for a fight. When I didn't give it to him, he hurled himself down the stairs to rail at my mother about me. For whatever reason, that night she stood up for me. The end result was a phone ripped from the wall, her screaming for me to call the police, my father chasing me through a snowbank to our neighbor's house, tasers, a night in jail, and a two-week restraining order.

On my father's return home, my mother seemed overjoyed that he'd agreed to counseling. I was told I would be attending with them, as this was a 'family problem.' It wasn't long after that I continued to hear how I contributed to and caused this 'family problem.' Among other things, I had embarrassed my father in front of the neighbors by running to them for help. When my parents went to France, I was told I wasn't going because I was such a terrible daughter.

Is it any surprise I was unhappy in my home? I excelled in academics, always on honor roll and in the National Honor Society. I excelled in music, buying and teaching myself to play a number of instruments, and playing in numerous school and community groups. I played in two top-notch youth symphonies, as well as being invited as a sophomore to play for my high school jazz band—a group that normally required auditions and took only the best musicians in the school.

My hopes to play professionally in a symphony orchestra and write novels were my light at the end of the tunnel. But there was another, stronger vision I had, that left me always believing God had plans for me; that God was with me no matter what.

My junior year of high school was also a time of choosing a college. While my older sister went to college because she was told she would, I had long wanted to earn a degree in music. This became another source of conflict, as my father—who had raised us from the time we could understand language to know we would go to college and we would pay for it ourselves—told me what I would and would not study. I would not get a degree in music, he told me—never mind that I would be the one paying for the degree. I would get a degree in something practical, something productive, something that would earn money.

My parents have, since I was in Kindergarten or younger, told me and anyone who will listen, that I am 'stubborn...just stubborn.' I don't think they were ever correct, at least not in their connotation. I think the truth is that I have always, from a young age, refused to back down when I know I'm speaking the truth or doing the right thing. I think the accusation that I was 'stubborn' first arose when, at the age of four, I told the truth of an adult's improper behavior and refused to make life easy by saying I'd lied. I had not.

Likewise, with my choice of study in college, I was not going to back down, because I knew, on a deep and profound level, that music was not merely something I *wanted* to do, not merely something I enjoyed. It was something God *called* me to do. I believed it then with my whole heart and soul and still do, today. I may not understand the reasons, but I believe He did, and it played into my choices then.

From the first time I picked up my grandfather's beautiful silver trombone, when I was 8, I loved the instrument. From the day I started playing in sixth grade, I knew I wanted to be a performing musician. I do not say 'know' lightly. I *knew*. And that knowledge has never changed.

I knew because of the stronger vision: When I was in late elementary school and early junior high, I sometimes heard heavenly music as I lay in bed at night. Yes, I heard it audibly. It was very soft, as if faint and far away; but audible and the most beautiful music you could imagine. I felt music so beautiful could only be of God and that if I was hearing it, I had a calling, even an obligation, to write what I was hearing. That meant studying music on a deeper level—earning a degree in it. And that's what I intended to do.

My father was a military officer with a temper that could be fearsome. Although my parents called me 'stubborn' I don't think anyone could accuse me of being belligerent, confrontational, or foolish. I would, if possible, avoid confrontation. I'd seen my father rip phones from walls. I'd seen him throw my older sister on a bed and choke her. I didn't want a fight with a full-grown man who could become violent.

Yet when he told me I would not major in music, I politely disagreed. I believed strongly enough in what I had experienced—and I still do, decades later—that my father was not going to move me from this goal.

I earned my way into the low brass department at a private university. I was overjoyed to be dropped off five hours from home and watch my parents drive away. In being out from under the constant criticism and anger at home, I felt a completely new person emerge. I felt more confident in myself, without the steady drumbeat of negativity and swearing and complaints and fault-finding I had lived with at home. I was free, and loving my life in college, playing trombone, making friends who weren't influenced in any way by my parents, and I was working toward my life's dream.

The year ended and I went home. As per my father's orders, I immediately had a job on returning home. I worked 30 hours a week, saving for college bills, and spent another ten or more hours a week practicing my instrument. I had good friends. I lived a clean life, straight as an arrow. No drinking, no drugs, no staying out late. I mostly stayed in my room.

But somehow, it wasn't good enough. I was supposed to be working 60 hours a week, not 30. I was supposed to somehow get along better with my younger sister. (On this matter I will only say, I believe even now that family dynamics made that an impossible task and the dynamics of an alcoholic family have created problems I cannot solve by myself.) I did my best simply to stay away from this sister, with whom there was invariably trouble, and was then blamed for *not* spending time with her. The upshot was that, in those six weeks, at the age of 18, my father repeatedly threatened to kick me out of the house.

I wish I could tell you what it is to be 18 and constantly threatened like that. I barely remember and in fact, I think I had a strong faith that led me to have the backbone my mother despised—in knowing I would find a way to deal with whatever came. I had tasted life outside of this criticism and started on my life's dream, and to the best of my memory, I had a certain confidence that somehow things would be okay.

Although memories aren't always completely clear years later, I think that even before the ax fell, I had begun to prepare. I spent hours in the library researching, and found there was a legal path to being declared financially independent of one's parents while still a minor. It would mean that my loans and grants would be based on my income, rather than my father's.

On July 5, 1987, there had been heavy rain in our town. As I had for several years, I set out to meet my friend Paul for our annual cruise on his family's yacht to celebrate his birthday. I had barely gotten to the end of our street when my car was swamped in deep water that washed up and flooded the spark plugs. It was a scene repeated all over the metro that morning and to dozens upon dozens of far more experienced drivers than I.

It didn't matter. I was to blame. I should have known this, I should have seen that—never mind that no one had ever taught me, to look for such things in heavy rain. My father railed and raged, demanded I buy the new plugs and change them out myself—the whole time as he reprimanded and chastised and accused me of foolishness and re-listed my many faults and threatened again to kick me out of the house if I didn't shape up.

I had just finished my first year at the most expensive college in its state. My father wasn't paying for it, but at least I wasn't paying rent for the summer. Still, the constant threat of being kicked out was too stressful.

When my parents went out of town for a funeral, I packed my things and left. I returned to my college, gave them every penny I had to cover summer rent and the next semester's tuition, completed the legal paperwork—which included statements from family members attesting that the problems in our family warranted a judge's decree and that I was genuinely financially on my own—and set to work at two jobs. In the morning and early afternoon I worked six to eight hours as a waitress at a small cafe in town. I walked back to my dorm room two blocks away, slept for a couple of hours, and got up to do another eight hours prepping for the chefs at a bigger restaurant at the far end of Central Avenue. I walked home late at night, slept three or four hours, and got up to do it all over again.

I did this for the rest of the summer, stepping out in faith that somehow I would get through the semester I had paid for and earn enough to pay for the next.

I can't say I distinctly remember praying and asking for God's help. But I know I did. The truth is, I was in a daze of exhaustion much of the time. To highlight how exhausted and unable to think clearly—there was a cook at one of the frat houses on campus. Her husband had, the year before, been released from jail, having done time for sexual crimes. On his release, he quickly became friendly with the college students. He showed up at my room one day claiming to have a potential job—to *help* me. He wanted to demonstrate how short the waitresses' skirts needed to be and how low their blouses needed to be by rolling up my skirt and tucking in my shirt. I remember being in a daze and thinking I needed to stop him and yet being in too much of an exhausted daze to process what was really happening. I think I must have finally backed away. I only know nothing happened.

Another day, he showed up at my room wanting to 'help' me again by making me breakfast in his and his wife's apartment. She was already out at her job. Convenient.

He suggested I take a bath to relax and he'd bring me breakfast in the tub. When I declined, he acted indignant that I might think he'd do anything. I remember being in such a daze of exhaustion as he led me out of my dorm, that I simply didn't seem to have any ability to formulate the word *No* or the energy to refuse. To this day, I don't remember if I ate breakfast there or left. But I didn't get in the tub and I know nothing happened.

When I look back on these incidents, I know God was there, protecting me. I was far too exhausted, emotionally, mentally, and physically, to protect myself. I know what that man was and I know he could easily have done anything he wanted—and had in the past. For some reason, he didn't.

Things did fall into place. My petition for legal independence was granted. I received grants and loans and finished college, entirely on my own from the time I was 18. By the time I graduated, furthermore, I was married and had a one-year-old son. Yet I finished college only a trimester after my classmates and with a good GPA.

In the years since, I've stepped out in faith in many ways. I've achieved my goals of playing music and writing novels—and done it while raising a large family. I've done very little composition and yet I still believe the heavenly music I used to hear was a clear road sign and promise to me, that brought me through a situation that should have left me, at the very least, unable to finish my degree, and at worst in some very dark places. The 'scapegoat' in alcoholic families often ends up living down to their assigned family role, involved in drugs, alcohol, casual sex, and worse. I absolutely believe it is by the grace of God and the heavenly music He gave me that I never went that direction.

Instead, miraculously—and I genuinely mean miraculously, knowing what I do of the average alcoholic family—I finished my degree and, in walking through that dark valley of exhaustion, no harm came to me.

Because of stepping out in faith to work in music, I have been led to works I may never have imagined. One of my current projects delves into the connection between our physical world and God, into seeing the importance of beauty in music and art, as given to us by God.

This and my other writing and music are part of what led me to a very blessed marriage. Today, I am seeing my children grow into very fine young men and women—ten in all. Among them: college degrees including a Ph.D., a soldier, a Marine, kids who work with horses and volunteer to help handicapped children.

Most importantly, they have great senses of humor and love each other. They love their new sisters- and brothers- in law and nephews being brought into the family and when we get together, there is a lot of love and laughter as we talk about our many fond memories. Do you remember when…? always followed by laughter.

It all stems from that early faith God gave me. I thank Him daily for that gift.

I sometimes wonder why He called me so strongly to music. Although I was fortunate enough to study composition with a very fine jazz composer, I haven't composed great works or done anything phenomenal in music, after all. But when I look back on the many ways He has guided and helped and protected me, starting with those gold-covered books and the sound of heavenly music, my faith only grows, that He had His plan for me, that I have prayed throughout the years, and He has continued to watch over me and protect me, no matter what happens.

If we turn to Him with our whole heart and soul, I believe He always will. The road may sometimes seem dark, but look ahead with faith, and He will be there.

Christine

Author, Composer, Musician, Mother
United States

Striving Despite Disappointments

ADAM PARR

If you want something you've never had, you must be willing to do something you've never done.
– Thomas Jefferson

My story begins back when I was 13 years of age, a time when I wasn't taking things seriously. I got involved with the wrong people. My ego was getting in the way. I had a lot of arrogance. I wasn't really thinking about where I was going and what I was doing.

Then, one summer's day during the school holidays, me and my friends decided to go climbing on roofs. This particular roof we climbed on was a church roof. Whilst on this roof, I climbed onto a skylight, unaware of what I was standing on.

Moments later the glass shattered. I fell through the skylights and onto a sink. I must have fallen fifteen feet. I had lacerations and had cut my arm open. I went into a state of shock. I thought I was going to die!

One of my friends raced through the door and helped me out. I ended up going to hospital, where I was checked over and kept for several hours before being released.

In the hospital they said I was lucky to be alive. I had no serious damage to any bones or tissue. An x-ray found no physical issues at all.

Over time, however, other issues arose. About a month after the fall, I began experiencing anxiety, depression, and PTSD. It happened whilst I was preparing for my GCSEs in my final year of secondary school.

Other things were happening, too, apart from the exams. The accident opened my eyes to the fact I'd been around the wrong kinds of people. I backed away from these friendships, and as a result, was goaded and targeted, alienated and victimized. I began to get into fights with these people. Each day I went to school with my defenses up, never knowing if I was going to have a fight.

Home was no better. My stepdad was very negative toward me. Between PTSD, depression, anxiety, a negative stepdad, and problems at school—including some teachers who were quite negative—it was one of the hardest times of my life.

There was one bright spot: My mother. She was in training to be a counselor and hypnotherapist. In addition to seeing a therapist and my doctor, I received hypnosis from my mother. All of it together really helped me push through this difficult time.

Still, as time went on, I continued to experience intense anxiety and thoughts and feelings that I was going to die. They were often triggered in crowded situations.

My first anxiety attack hit me when I was taking an exam. I froze and couldn't finish the exam. My frustration grew and I often questioned, *Why me? Why is this happening to me?*

But over time, with therapy and working through these things, I began to find understanding. The anxiety, PTSD, and depression disappeared.

In looking back, I feel that time in my life ultimately made me stronger as a human being and enabled me to really tune into my own awareness. I developed empathy for other people and how they feel. I developed a strong desire to help other people struggling with their mental health.

I left school. I went to college and did a B. Tech national diploma in public services. My first aim was to join the military and become a policeman, but I ended up trying many routes of education and lines of work. None, it seemed were for me. I decided to go to university to study criminology. That also wasn't for me. So I enrolled in a course to become a life coach. I qualified in 2019, in December.

This is something I still do today and am building on. I created a podcast in January 2020. During the Covid lock down, I produced 80 podcasts. I've connected with lots of amazing people. My podcast focuses on self-development, positivity mind-set, mental health, and much more. The podcast has grown dramatically in this short time. I'm humbled and grateful for all the connections I've made and the positive value I've brought to other people.

My goals in life are to have a positive impact on other people; to be the best I can be to help other people be the best they can be; to always strive to be the best version of myself and to have a positive impact on others in the world; to be a public speaker, life coach, and to be successful in life.

I believe we have the ability to create whatever we want to create if we see it to as possible. And it is possible —through believing in yourself and growing in your life; by pushing through your comfort zones and never settling for less than what you're capable of achieving. If something doesn't challenge you, you're not going to grow. We have to learn to get comfortable with being uncomfortable. We are not designed to settle for a mediocre life. We are designed to push out of our comfort zones, and to develop ourselves as human beings.

I want to leave the reader with the profound quote

that helped me in my life from A.A Mine. "You are braver that you believe, and stronger that you seem, and smarter that you think."

Go and conquer your mountain and strive to achieve your dreams and passions in life. There is nothing impossible for God. Just allow Him to lead you!

Adam Parr
Life coach,
Host of The Parrsitivity Podcast,
Motivational speaker
United Kingdom

The One that Just Won't Quit

BRENDA WANJIRU

As I see it, motivational speakers never tell the full stories of how they became successful. Most of them leave out the most important part, the battle of the mind, how they convinced themselves they could do what they did. I am not a motivational speaker, but I am successful. No, I do not have a multi-billion dollar company and there's not much you'll find out about me when you search my name on Google. My success lies in having won a lot of mind battles.

Within my first month of Arabic class at the mosque, I was ready to throw in the towel. It had been one month of struggle and confusion. To be completely honest, I'd sit in class for two hours, watch everyone ask and answer questions, then leave once class was over. I did this every day for a month. "Why are you here? What have you done to yourself? You can always leave." I was the only non-Muslim in my class. I had to start with the alphabet, which was not the case for everyone else. They were all familiar with Arabic writing.

It was my mother's idea to study Arabic. She was and still is big fan of languages. She is a tad fluent in French and Arabic and seeing that she's a teacher, she speaks fluent English and Swahili and of course our mother tongue, Kikuyu, which is spoken in Kenya. So when I struggled to understand anything in Arabic class, I did not dare inform her. On the surface, I was very happy to tell anyone who cared that I was studying Arabic, but inside, I was terrified of failing my Arabic exams. Exams were offered after every three months of learning. I still had two months to make up my mind and yet, every day was horrific for me. One fine Tuesday morning, I stood in front of my mirror and said, "C'mon Brenda, we need to make a decision. Are we in or out? It's either you do it and excel or you leave and try something else." I stood there, for about 23 minutes. I knew I had to make a decision. Time was running out.

I was studying for my Bachelor of Education (Arts) at the University of Nairobi at the time and the work load was a nightmare. I'd give myself a pep talk every day, standing in front of the mirror. "Brenda, you're ready for today, you're smart and courageous, look at you doing big things with your life." I don't know how I came to find out that using the mirror was that effective. Of course, I'd make sure no one ever found me talking to myself—that would be weird!

And so I decided to walk into that mosque, a scared young non-Muslim girl who was, nonetheless brave enough and strong enough to risk looking stupid in the eyes of others and ready to fail, to be poor at something and maybe be disappointed.

Now, I hold amazing transcripts. These papers tell a story of success, but the real story lies in my mind, the hard work and sacrifice it took. I owe it to myself to live the greatest life I'm capable of living, even if that means I have to be alone for a very long time. I love the words of Heidi Preibe: *The future we want will not arrive without our participation.*

So close your eyes and take a deep breath, visualize where you want to be and what you want to have; see it and smell it and make it real for yourself. Now work toward that.

Recently, I was diagnosed with goiter. It's one of those conditions that sneak into your body. When I stand in front of the mirror to give myself the usual pep talk, I stretch my neck and see that I have another battle to fight. Then come the negative thoughts that want to put you down. They go like this, "If you don't achieve your goals, you have an excuse. You're sick!" But I've seen people with chronic illnesses achieve more. I've seen people with no limbs doing more. I've seen people, with much less than I have, get up every morning and choose to fight and aspire to win this battle of the mind.

I submit my worries to the Almighty. He has seen me through the most difficult situations, like when my parents split up, when I lost my government sponsorship to study Pharmacy, when I had to take a gap year before going to campus, when I lost three of my grandparents to cancer and one to blood pressure complications, when I lost a dear friend to suicide. There are people out there with longer lists of all the hardships they have gone through. How we allow these situations to affect us is what matters most. What goes through your mind when you're hurting?

Recently got your heart broken? You have to mourn the loss of something you thought would last forever. Lost a really good job? Regret not having gone wilder in your twenties? What if I told you that nothing was ever meant to last forever? You're happy for a while, but you can't hold onto that forever, you have to let it go for it to mean something. Every event is a lesson, your thoughts about this lesson are what will change everything at the end of the day. If you see yourself as a victim, guess what? You will be a victim. If you see yourself a victor, a survivor, a strong-willed, witty fellow, then you will be exactly that.

I met up with my mentor some time back. I was

feeling rather discouraged. I was feeling left out. I thought everything in my life was getting delayed. Most of my classmates and friends were already enjoying the fruits of their labor, they were (and still are) taking vacations and it was hard to watch. For a moment there, I thought doing what they did would be an assurance of getting to where they are. I thought doing an accounting course like Amy would give me exactly what Amy had—great hair, great boyfriend, great job, great house. Or maybe studying law like Kate would get me to where Kate is. I was willing to disown my dreams. I was in a rush to reach a destination I wasn't sure existed.

After I had finished complaining and threatening to change my career, my mentor asked me, "Are you going to be proud of this decision five years from now when things will have gone south? Don't you think it's less exhausting to be yourself?" There it was. Who exactly was I? Was I the type to deviate from a path I had chosen simply because I couldn't see through the fog?

These are the battles of the mind. The world is full of flashy and attractive distractions. There will always be someone taller, luckier, smarter, richer, and happier than you. You may get fed up of doing the same thing every day with no success, and that's fine. What do you tell yourself? Do you scold yourself? Do you think you're enough? Are you scared that you're not? I cannot tell you what to think. Others choose to trick their enemies, others choose to be more strategic and send out spies first. It doesn't matter how you get it done, just win the battle. If you have to study ten hours to pass the test, do it. If you have to make time for the gym before work, do it. I choose to go the extra mile every day, and to learn about the lies the devil keeps telling me to make me doubt myself.

I know I'm not as smart as Albert Einstein, I might not be the best linguist to have ever lived, but I most definitely will not be the worst.

I will not be a coward. Being scared is a good thing. If I'm terrified of my dreams, it means I have big dreams, I know I am on the right track, I know that being comfortable where I am now will do nothing good for me. So yes, I will go ahead and register for dance class, I will apply for that job I think I'm not qualified for, I will pitch my ideas to the partners, I will do the things that terrify me.

What's the worst that could happen? I'd rather try than sit here wondering what could have happened if only I'd tried. We regret more the things we didn't do than the ones we actually did. Choose your battles wisely, and most importantly, win.

Brenda Wanjiru
Language Enthusiast

Kenya

Losing My Mother

NICOLE BIANCHI D'ANNA

"But you, Lord, are a compassionate and gracious God, slow to anger, abounding in love and faithfulness." – Psalm 86:15

Life is not always easy. We go through good and bad times. We are either in a valley or on a mountain. Life can get messy. I call the mess a "puddle." You are either in the puddle, jumping over the puddle, or you have a toe touching the puddle, but the puddle is always there. That is life. My dad would always tell me, "Nicole, life is not always easy, but that's life, and you must find ways to deal with it. You cannot give up and hide from your problems." He was right. You are going to have to deal with many challenges in life. However, with faith, prayer and love, change will come when you are in the puddle. And that change is necessary for you to grow and become closer to the Lord.

No matter if you are in deep waters or stepping around it, God is present and loving you. Throughout my entire life, I have gone through several exceedingly difficult situations and God has been there. I may not have noticed Him while I was in the puddle, but as I reflect on those difficult times, He was always there loving me. Sometimes, He guided me and gave me the knowledge and grace to get through those tough times. Sometimes, He worked through others and sometimes He carried me. But He was always there loving me. And in the end, that change that occurred in me was what I really needed, and further, it brought me closer to Him.

I believe prayer is so powerful. Prayer is not just for asking God for things or trying to negotiate with Him. Prayer can be used to talk to Him, to share your thoughts with Him, to tell Him you love Him, and that you are so thankful and grateful to Him. I believe that through prayers, listening to Him, and following what He says, you can change the situation you are in. I know this because He has answered so many of my prayers throughout my life. I worship Him in the morning when I get up, while I am doing my chores around the house and when I go to sleep. I talk to Him when I am nervous and to thank Him for all His blessings. Prayer is how I communicate with Him. I seek Him out all day long. I know He is listening. I hear Him inside of me. He is filled with love.

My mother, Nicoletta Bianchi, was born in Italy and came to the United States when she was 12 years old.

She married my father, Nicholas, and had three children, Joseph, Anthony, and me. We are a remarkably close, affectionate, loving family. Our closeness has been envied by so many friends and family members. My mother and father were hard working people. My mother was a strong woman with a remarkable work ethic.

We were a middle-class family and my brothers and I were my parents' number one priority. My parents sacrificed everything to send us to private elementary, middle, and high schools so we could have the best education. They were our biggest fans and advocates. They never missed a football game, baseball game, dance recital, floor hockey game, bowling tournament, soccer game, or cheerleading event, ever.

Our house was "the house" where all our friends came to eat, sleep, and laugh. There was nothing my mom's home cooking couldn't fix. My mom was the heart of our house. She was the glue that held our family together. She was an incredibly quiet woman, with a dry sense of humor. She was filled with love and compassion for her family and everyone she met. She never spoke negatively about a single human being. She would give the shirt off her back to help anyone out. Her soul-filling food, love, and compassion is the reason why I started a free monthly meal at my church for approximately eight years. She would say to me, "Nicole, there are a lot of lost souls out there." She had the biggest heart and loved deeply and sincerely. She was not only my mother, but my best friend, and we were awfully close throughout her entire life. When I was diagnosed with a thyroid disorder and two auto-immune diseases, my mother was there, researching, getting me into the best doctors and always taking care of me when I did not feel like I could get off the couch. She was always there. Everyone who knew her, knew she was one of a kind. She was the best and she was my best friend. That was my mom.

We knew my mother's health was turning for the worse around 2018, about two years before she died. During that time, my mom was in ICU. She suffered a mini stroke, and one of the doctors called me to say he thought she only had a few months left to live. When I heard that news, I was terrified I was going to lose her. I prayed. And you know what? He heard those prayers and answered them. She lived for two more years. Do you see what prayers can do?

As soon as she got out of the ICU and came home, a close family friend got her an appointment to see his cardiologist. At first, my mother was hesitant, but I took her and told her we need another opinion. I wanted to fight for her just like she had fought for me. Her new cardiologist gave her phenomenal care and she lived for two more years—two more years filled with memories for my entire family and me.

My mom passed on Saturday, June 13, 2020 around 5:30 pm. She passed during the year of the pandemic. On Friday, the day before she passed, while grocery shopping with my dad, my mom's ICU doctor contacted us. She had gone to the hospital early Thursday morning, around 2:00 am, because she woke up speaking incomprehensibly and unable to move. My brother, Joe, immediately called 911 and the ambulance came and took her to the hospital. Neither my brother nor my father could go with her because of the pandemic. When the doctor called on my dad's cell phone, we were stunned. She was talking to us about my mom's last wishes and how her body was shutting down.

Wait, how was this happening? My mind started racing. I just took her to her cardiologist on Wednesday, a few days ago, and they told her she may need dialysis. Her legs had swelled up and she had put on a lot of water weight. Her heart was too weak to pump the fluid out, and therefore, her legs were weeping with water from her pores. Water would drip from her legs onto the floor. This scared my brother and me enormously. I had never seen this before. I followed her and my brother, Joe, back to their house and spent the afternoon with her, cooking, cleaning, hugging, and holding her hand while she slept on her chair, covered with a mound of blankets because she was always cold.

On Thursday evening, while she was at the hospital,

my children and I spoke to her on the phone. She told us she loved all of us. She sounded good. My youngest daughter said, "Nana, you need to come home so you can come over and make us your soup." Hearing her little voice always brought joy to my mother. My head was spinning.

As we stood in the corner of the store, the doctor explained that my mother did not want to be kept alive by machines. My mom told the doctor I would fight to stop them from taking her off, but it was what she wanted. Did my mom know this was the end?

People kept walking by us in the store, carrying on their own conversations and shopping; life was moving forward, and I was trying to pull it together and not scream, especially in front of my dad. She was "my" mother, but she was my dad's wife and love for over 50 years. What happened in the last 24 hours that got us to this point? I was baffled.

I knew at this point that my mom's life was coming to an end and I could not go to see her, hug her, or kiss her. She was in the hospital, alone, without her family. We could not be there to advocate for her, to make sure she was comfortable, to ask questions, to make sure she was being taken care of. We weren't there. I felt so conflicted. I wanted her to stay alive, but I knew she had been suffering far too long. She was so weak and would lay on her chair almost the whole of the day. It took so much energy for her to sit at the table and eat with my dad. She was mentally and physically exhausted. To watch this tough woman become so weak was frightening. I was so nervous to think my mom's life was coming to an end here on earth.

I started praying while we were in the store. I prayed for God to give me the strength for what I was about to face—the loss of my mother. I thanked Him for the time He gave us together. I prayed He would take her quickly and bring her home to Heaven. I prayed if this was His will, that it be done His way. I prayed He would take her in the palm of His hand and guide her to heaven. I knew in my heart she was ready to meet Christ, our Father. She had suffered a lot throughout those last two years. I didn't want her to be in any more pain. I was blessed the Lord gave me that time with her.

At the end of my mom's life, I was not able to be in the room with her in the ICU because of the pandemic. We could only have two family members. My dad asked me to be there. I prayed about this and something inside me told me it should be my brother, Joe. This was difficult to hear because I knew I would not be able to see her before she passed. However, I told my dad Joe was the one who needed to be with her the most during her final moments.

He was right. My brother had a lot of things he

wanted to tell my mother before she left this world. Joe needed to find peace within himself before she passed. Joe had moved in with my parents to care for my mother over the last year. She loved all of us, but Joe really was her favorite. My other brother, Tony, and I parked outside the hospital and watched on Facetime as my mother received her last rites and got ready to meet Our Lord and Savior in heaven. It was horrible that we could not be with her. It was horrible that we had to watch my mom's end of life from a parking lot inside a car. It was horrible that we could not touch her, hold her, comb her hair, kiss her, or see her face to face before she went home to Heaven. Tony and I cried in the car together, watching our mother lie there. I will never forget that image of my mom in that hospital room. However, it was supposed to be like that. It was God's will.

After the minister blessed my mother, I screamed "Stop. Maybe she'll be okay now." For a moment, I had hope that she would fight through this and come home. However, my dad knew it was time. He said, "No, Nicole. She's not okay." From 11:30 on that Saturday morning until 4:30 in the afternoon, we watched my brother and my father surround my mother with love, hugs, touches, kisses, and beautiful words spoken to her, as opera, her favorite music, played in her room. Around 4:30 pm, my father called me on my cell phone when my brother, Joe, had stepped out of the room to get a bottled water. My dad said, "Nicole, I think you need to get Joe to leave. Maybe ask him to get a bite to eat. I think your mom is trying to pass, and I think she's waiting for Joe to leave."

So, Tony and I called Joe and asked him to come with us to our mom and dad's house to get a quick bite to eat. We told him he could bring a dish of food back for dad, too. He agreed. He followed us in his car and we met at my parent's house. It seemed as soon as we all walked in the door, the phone rang. We looked at the phone and Joe grabbed it. Tony and I watched our brother's eyes close and his face flatten, and we knew what had just happened. My dad was on the other end and had just told Joe our mother's soul had passed to heaven.

At first, I was in awe and then I just cried uncontrollably while hugging my brothers. My brothers and I were all together in her house when she died. That is how she would have wanted it. I know that is how God wanted it. I know that for certain. However, I could not believe she died without all of us there surrounding her with our love. I was with her throughout my whole life and I desperately wanted to be there at the end of hers and I was not. She was the one I turned to every time. She was the one I told everything to. She never judged me. She always told me I am human and flawed and that was okay. She was my biggest fan but would not hold back to give constructive criticism when needed. She was so proud that I was a lawyer, business owner, married for 25 years, and had four children. She was proud that my family was my number one priority, like hers was. She always worried about my family and me, but now she was gone. Now, who was going to be there for me? Who would worry about me? Who would I talk to a thousand times a day? Who was going to tell me everything was going to be okay? I just wanted my mom back just for a little while longer. Just one more kiss. Just one more hug. Just one more "I love you." Just let me hold her, hold her hand, touch her one more time.

Then I thought, this is how the Lord wanted this. He is in control. I felt selfish for wanting more time even though she was so sick. She had suffered so much throughout the past two years. She was in a puddle. She would tell me there was no dignity in being this sick. I would tell her Christ had no dignity hanging on the cross for us and that she was going to be okay. She was humiliated that her husband and children had to bathe her, feed her, and take care of her. We were honored to do it for her. However, she felt defeated.

I prayed and prayed every day she was alive. I thanked God for his blessing every day and I asked Him to give her strength mentally and physically. I asked Him to make her feel better, to give her more time with the kids and me. He did all of that. How could the Lord love me this much?

I believe the Lord brought her home to heaven, so she didn't have to suffer anymore. No more pain. No more hospitals. No more feeling humiliated or weak or without dignity. No more. It was time. I also believe the Lord knew how much I emotionally depended on my mother throughout my life and that I was okay to be on my own now as a wife, mother, daughter, and sister. This was His will. He knew I would be devastated, but was resilient enough to be okay. And He knows how I love Him and how I will serve Him my whole life.

After she passed and days went by, I struggled to find a sign from her that she was okay. Everyone who has a loved one pass always talks about these signs they get from them. Why didn't my mom give me a sign? But after thinking about this, I wondered, do I really need a sign? I knew she was in Heaven with our Lord. I know this.

Then, one night I went outside while my husband played with our two dogs and something plopped on my head. It was bird poop. Now why would this remind me of my mom? Because the last time I got pooped on was on my honeymoon, 25 years ago. I had immediately called my mom from the Dominican Republic and she said it was good luck to get pooped on by a bird. I knew this was a sign from my mom.

Months have passed and I continue my daily prayers.

Although losing my mom was devastating, my faith in the Lord gave me the strength to get through that "puddle." As I reflect on everything that has happened, I believe God, through others, helped me get through this difficult time too. I felt *loved* from so many people—family members, friends, and acquaintances. People reached out with love. They sent cards, flowers, special gifts, and food; they called, texted, and messaged. I will be forever grateful and thankful to Him and to everyone who loved and supported my family and me throughout this time.

"Whoever does not love does not know God, because God is love." – 1 John 4:8

"So now faith, hope and love abide, these three; but the greatest of these is love.". Prayers, Faith, Hope and Love to all of you. – 1 Corinthians 13:13

Nicole Bianchi D'Anna
Lawyer
Business Owner
Wife and mother
United States

A.S.K. and He Will Answer

DR. TAMARA MATTISON

In 1988 I lost my father to cancer. By 1993 I lost my mother to diabetes complications. After my father's death I did not grieve but instead medicated myself with drugs and became an addict for five years. While I was in my addiction I attended Friendship West Baptist Church in Dallas, Texas. By 1993 my mom's death made me cry out to God, which he answered and said, Come unto me all who are heavy laden, and I will give you rest! (Matt 11:28) I began my sold-out relationship with God and have not looked back! I've seen God take me from drug addiction and domestic violence through a journey of healing and deliverance. All along the way God has been faithful to walk with me, which led me to have the faith in Him that I share today!

God has allowed me to have many miracles, signs, and wonders over the past twenty-six years and I can't thank Him enough. As a woman of God, I faced many devils that tried to destroy my hope and faith in Him, but the word of God is quick, and powerful, and sharper than any two-edged sword, piercing even to the dividing asunder of soul and spirit, and of joints and marrow, and is a discerner of the thoughts and intents of the heart. (Hebrews 4:12)

I had the blessed opportunity to open the first Safe Harbor Shelter for girls ages 12-17, called Brittany's Place, in the state of Minnesota in 2014! I prayed the whole time for God's direction in creating a holistic model of care that included reunification of these girls with their families. After 2 ½ years the organization got a new CEO who eliminated my position and I was removed from some of the most amazing ministry I partook of in my life. I was devastated and yet God, who is faithful and just, kept me during those times of depression. My Pastor Wayne Randolph Felton ministered to me and let me know that God was not done with me yet!

The first lesson I learned was that I had begun to be busy with the work and less busy in prayer! I was dying a slow death in my prayer life and relationship with God due to making my job an idol!

Lesson number two was that God is a jealous God and he will not allow his people to have any idols.

Today as I walk in one of the most amazing opportunities as the Assistant Divisional Social Service Director for the Salvation Army, I know God will keep my mind, body, and soul as I keep my prayer life active. I went from being on welfare in 1994 to obtaining my Doctorate degree in Organization Management with a specialization in Leadership in 2013! God is a great God and he is greatly to be praised!

Dr. Tamara Mattison
Organization Management with Specialization in Leadership
United States

Finding God in the Small Miracles

HARRIS JARRAL

"Truly I tell you, if you have faith as small as mustard seed, you can say to this mountain, 'move from here to there,' and it will move. Nothing will be impossible for you. — Matthew 17:20

Miracles work when you are focused and sometimes even when you are not prepared for them. Let me share three stories: one story from one day and two from another. On Tuesday September 1, 2020 I saw two miracles.

One week before that Tuesday, on Wednesday, August 26, a girl I had known for six years asked me for some help regarding money. I checked out my accounts and found I had only 3000 rupees. So, keeping myself a bit safe, I offered her 2000 but asked if I could give them to her on Monday. She agreed and I prayed that her issue be sorted out by God somehow on Sunday.

The rest of my week, through the weekend, was quite

busy and by Monday I had forgotten all about her. Tuesday was occupied with work in the studio, until late at night. Before I left the studio, my partner handed me more than 3000 rupees. Without that, I had only Rs 350. I had forgotten my promise and spent it.

When I got home from my studio I received her WhatsApp message. "Harris u didn't get back to me. I'm waiting for ur text."

I replied "Yes, please share your account details so I can transfer you the money."

She asked me about a few ways we might transfer money by bank, card, online or other platforms. I was thinking how on Tuesday night I received another Rs 3000 for myself whereas the old Rs 3000 was well spent without even remembering or making any effort to fulfill that promise. So I was glad to have her text message late at night. She still needed the money and was so grateful to me because she couldn't ask anyone from her home and she had left her job in lockdown.

Then the girl asked me, "Can I ask you a question?" She started to talk about a medical problem she was dealing with, and some dreams she had.

I told her healing is always from the Lord and if she can forgive everyone for God's sake, she can heal her spirit and her spirit will heal her body. In the end, she said she didn't need any money and she felt good without it or any medical checkups or treatments.

On that same day we were waiting for a friend who was coming from another city to a celebration dinner. He had to meet a friend who lived in a town between his and ours, on his way to see us. We had called him several times, as everyone expected him at anytime. Then a bell rang. My heart told me it's him on the door. But it was the building's security guard. He had come before to deliver something but nobody was there to collect it before. I had just reached for my phone to check with my friend how far he was when I heard a loud *Hello* from the friend we all were waiting for.

I became really grateful to God for such blessings that He even sends you everyday, all the time, in such quick manifestations. God's love and grace is always by our side. Either we are focused or not. His blessings come whether you believe it or not, but believing and focus always work as a catalyst.

The last short story is from this month. I came home one early morning on a summer day. I was exhausted and ready to hit my bed but my security guard told me there had been a spark in the electric meter because some cat had jumped on it. Luckily, the cat was fine, but the wires were not. They had gotten sparked up and now there was no light before you come in. There was no electricity and as the sun rose—so would the heat. You need to complain to the electricity complaint centre, the security guard told me.

Up in my room, I called the complain centre. So began the long wait for their answer. The attendant told me the team was busy resolving other complaints. It would likely take two or three hours to reach my home. If they got free soon, however, they would call me back. I could only wait and wonder—would the electric be out for a long time or would it begin to work? I was getting worried and sleepy and my frustration grew.

Then an idea flashed came to me. I tried to clear my mind of all the thoughts. As I did, I felt peace in my head. Sleep spread, surrounding my legs, ears, and everywhere.

Somewhere in that calm, I heard the tiny beeping sound of the air conditioner turning on. The electricity was back. The light was back in the house—and I didn't know how. The beloved God had sent His blessings and I had a peaceful sleep.

The bigger remains the bigger, the bigger God knows about you. Now you need to understand what you can do to change and he can tell you what to do. Separations and illusion are all a mind game. You belong to him. He loves you.

"O My servants who have transgressed against themselves (by sinning), Do not despair of the mercy of Allah. Indeed, Allah forgive all sins. Indeed, it is he who is the Forgiving, The Merciful. And return to your lord and submit to him." — Quran 39:53

Harris Jarral

Singer / Song Writer

God always surrounds us and his love and mercy is for all at all the stages of life.

Pakistan

My First Love

SALIHA

Someone asked me a couple of years ago, "How was it when you fell in love the first time?" And this would take me back to the very first relationship I had.

As with many 16-year-olds, it was a time when I felt ready for giving and receiving love, or maybe deep inside I craved to be loved in that certain way a woman loves a man and a man loves a woman. It was the 90's and finding that true love to spend your life with was a dream of many of my friends. The problem was that I had very low self-esteem and so, I fell in love with the first man who said, "I love you," as if it was a contract that bonded us together forever and I was under the notion that you only fall in love once and that's that. He told me to keep it a secret and I agreed.

What followed was a disturbing two years where I was under the illusion of love, yet what I experienced was mostly mental pain and agony. I can say that I painfully sacrificed a lot for his happiness on a daily basis. It was as if I craved his approval when he was angry or unhappy. I could not bear to see him sad and yearned to hear him say that he loved me. Yet he used this power he had over me, under the guise of love, as a way to make me do things I did not want to do. Worse—I let him.

There came a point where I lost my voice and my ability to speak up. I was more like a slave to him in my head and the few times I saw my errors, he would call me back by manipulating me again and I would go back to him. I let him use me, just yearning to hear him say, "I love you." It was as if I was under a spell to do as he pleased but he used "love" as a form of manipulation while I did things for him that could give one shivers.

Often, I heard from common friends that he made fun of me with his mates, that he told everyone how foolish I was, how I would do anything for him, yet nothing felt true to my deaf ears. It was as though I had signed my fate with his and envisioned myself living a life of pain and misery under the guise of "love." Or maybe I believed my fate was sealed to the man who touched me first.

Looking back, I don't remember every little thing. It feels like broken memories. What I do remember clearly is the day he was coming to see me, and I suddenly had morbid thoughts, wishing—even hoping—he would have an accident or die before getting to my place. I was not brave enough to stop him from coming to me. That is the day my inner being started waking up a little and started telling me I needed to get out of this as soon as possible.

It was around then that I sought refuge in prayer. I started praying to God to help me. Still, due to the religious dogma and belief systems with which I was raised, I saw things from my own limited point of view. I did not feel worthy of "goodness" and I felt sinful or bad for having done the things I did with him and for his "love." I felt I was at fault and I was not happy in my own body. I remember crying on my prayer mat and feeling broken. I began to see that even in my disconnectedness from God, I was still connected to God. God was the only one to whom I had made all my confessions.

A few traumatic events later, I broke it off. After two years of letting my mind, body, and soul be used by someone, I finally ended it. The day I was done, I suddenly started becoming aware of all I had put up with for so long. What followed were suicidal thoughts and extreme pain. I went for a swim and had thoughts of drowning myself; I walked up steps and wondered how it would be if I just fell down the stairs; I watched the walls in my room and wondered if banging my head on the wall would make any difference to the profound pain I felt… where I felt trapped inside my own body.

I felt as if I was broken, inside out, and cut up into tiny pieces. There was immense torture within my body, mind, and soul. On the outside I looked okay but inside I was torn and broken. No one noticed. No one knew. I decided to bury it all and that helped me disconnect from the situation at the time.

One day I realized I may be broken in many ways, but my soul is mine and my soul is intact. From then on, it was my connection with the positive "God feeling" inside me, the divine messages I got through the music I listened to and danced to, and making new friends, that kept me alive. I started being there for others and it felt good to be purposeful and to be that friend to them.

In a way, the same religious beliefs that made me feel "sinful" also helped me not to take my life as suicide is strictly prohibited in the faith I follow. My real inner power arose the day I connected to the feeling of the God "within me." This feeling gave me a new sense of the world as I realized that no matter what I went through, I was always protected and loved by a bigger source that loves me unconditionally.

Recently I came across a saying by the amazing spiritual teacher Teal Swan. She says, "We are all Victims of Victims," and this helped me forgive myself. I was eventually able to forgive him, too, as part of the process of experiencing several spiritual awakenings in my life.

Now, many years later, in the year 2020, if someone asked me again, "How was it when you fell in love the first time?" I would say that I fell in love the day I came into this world from the non-physical to the physical and that is the day I was truly, madly, and deeply in love. This love is the light of God within me and I am excited to experience unconditional love within and outside of myself. To love all that is "me" inside out.

I am my very own "first love" and grateful to the universe that I am able to see that today.

Saliha
Filmmaker, soul coach.
Australia

The Value of
Our Name

ILONA PARUNAKOVA

I'll never forget the day my grandpa passed away when I was ten. I was excited because this meant I would finally be baptized. According to the Orthodox tradition all immediate family members, including grandchildren, must be baptized in order for a deceased's soul to enter heaven. Myself, my sister and five cousins had remained unbaptized. Now we would finally be initiated into our faith!

Armenian Orthodox tradition requires that anyone who is baptized receive a new Christian name. This excited me and my cousins—all who were girls. Each of us wanted a popular Christian name such as 'Armine,' Ripsime,' or 'Gayane.' Once at the church, the priest who was performing the baptism, who would assign our new names, looked at my parents and asked, "Who is that girl?" He pointed straight at me. "Is she Armenian?" I knew why he asked. He expected to see a girl with olive-colored skin, dark hair and dark eyes. He didn't know what name to give me since he had never seen an

Armenian girl with light skin, blonde hair and blue eyes like I had, inherited from my Ukrainian mom. The priest spent a few minutes in silence, reflecting. Then he spoke my new Christian name out loud. 'Lucine.' It was a name I had to use for forty days, and when I did, I felt different. I felt proud.

Our name is a key part of our identity. When we hear our name spoken out loud, we should feel good, as if the combination of syllables creates the most pleasant sound. When we are named by our parents our existence is confirmed; our name gives us a sense of value. We hear our name from childhood and associate it with our personality. Our name includes every part of us, our appearance and spiritual qualities, our feelings and emotional intelligence and our abilities and skills.

When someone addresses us by name, they bring attention to us, expressing respect and recognition of our importance and individuality. As we grow up some us may begin to associate our name with pleasant memories from our childhood whether it's the love and approval we received from our mother or other family members or an inner spiritual comfort and warmth. Hearing another person speak our name can cause us to feel pleasant emotions and place us in a positive mood where we can more easily feel sympathy, trust, and respect for another person we talk to.

Now, as I look back on my own journey, I can see how prophetic, powerful and profound my Christian name has been and how it has shaped my life; it has correlated perfectly with my given name—Ilona—which means Happiness and Joy, as if someone in Heaven had planned this all out for me! The two names together create an unexplainable synergetic and explosive divine power that has been a guiding force all my life.

My Christian name, Lucine, which means "the light," I received from the priest at the baptism has carried me through some of my darkest moments. I feel empowered when my name is spoken out loud, and I understand it's meaning; no matter how hard we try, we cannot get rid of darkness because it does not exist. 'For you are all children of light, children of the day. We are not of the night or of the darkness.' (Thessalonians 5:5). Darkness is nothing but the absence of light. In order to affect darkness, we must do something with light, because light is the only thing that actually exists.

Because I've been given a name that literally means 'light,' I feel the light in me that is me even more. My name gives me the strength in knowing I can affect any darkness I may feel because the intersection of light and darkness—and where light begins, is where miracles happen. This I know is true. I have experienced it in my own life. This is also the gift I bring into the world. God gave me my name to describe who I am. My name is a key part of my identity and why I came into this world, and what I am to contribute to iit—as our name is for all of us.

As we read the Bible, we find a huge number of names in it that are familiar to most of us. Yet do we know their true meaning? We may recognize names in the Bible such as Jesus, Mary, Adam, and Peter. Some even call their children by these names, often without knowing what the name means or what events they are associated with. The Bible though tells us that a name was given to a person for a reason, regardless of its beauty or popularity at the given time. The Bible explains that every name has a special meaning, which should manifest itself in the life of the person who received it. For example, in 1 Samuel 1:20, the Bible says, 'After some time Anna conceived and bore a son and gave him the name Samuel, for, [she said], I asked him from the Lord.' And indeed, the Hebrew name Shamuel, transformed into a more understandable Samuel, means 'shemua-el', that is, 'heard by God.' In the Bible we read Samuel's story and see how he became one of the greatest men of God in the Old Testament. This is truly an example of how the gift of the meaning of our name can show up in our life.

There are cases in the Bible where a person took one name from his parents, and then the Lord Himself gave them a new one and a new ministry. As in one such story, a boy who had a penchant for cunning received the name Jacob. This name is derived from 'akav', the root underlying the noun 'akev'–'heel' – and the verb 'akav,' that is 'to stammer, deceive, mislead.' In Gen. 25:26 the Bible says, 'Then his brother went out, his hand clutching Esau's heel; and his name was called Jacob. But after a period of testing Jacob received a new name from God— Israel!' As the Bible continues in Gen. 32: 28, 'And he said: henceforth your name will not be Jacob, but Israel, for you fought with God, and you will prevail over men.' The origin of the name Israel means, 'God will fight, fight', and also, 'God fights'. This is another example of how the meaning of our name has a deeper connection to the purpose of our life.

There are nearly three thousand different names in the bile, most which are related to the period of the Old Testament. As the influence of Christianity spread throughout the world, the popularity of Biblical names grew and over time became even more popular such as the two classical Biblical names, John and Mary. These same names are also found in other religions but colored in that particular nation's sound or tone. In Islam we find many familiar names: Ibrahim - Abraham; Musa - Moses, Yakub - Jacob, Yusuf - Joseph, Harun - Aaron, Ilyas - Elijah, Maryam - Mary, Isa - Jesus.

When we understand the meaning of a Biblical name, we understand the person more who was given it and

187

possibly even the motivation of the parent as to why they chose that particular name for their child. In addition, understanding the meaning of names can help us to better chose a name for our own children.

Scientists still cannot agree on some names; in such cases, different versions of the meaning are given. The task was also not set to reveal the meaning of absolutely all names. The selection contains only the most important and interesting names.

As I grew up, people asked me where my given name 'Ilona' came from. I too wondered but didn't know. Now I realize how much I do care to know the meaning behind my name given to me by my birth parents. Names hold importance for all of us; they are who we are, and they are the mark of our identity, with each name special and unique. When we honor our name we mind our actions, since right actions helps our name to be remembered in a good way, so we can leae a positive legacy.

In my early twenties I moved to Finland to study in the Seminary. In one of our weekly choir rehearsals, I bumped into a girl who asked me what my name was. "My name is Ilona," I replied as I introduced myself. There seemed no limit to this girl's excitement as she rapidly disclosed to me the meaning of my name. She said it was a Finish name meaning 'Joy and Happiness carrier.' In that moment I heard the phrase my dad used to say to me all the time when he addressed me—"My Joy," he'd say as he smiled. That's what my father had called me my entire life. I was his JOY!

The meaning of my name struck at my heart. I knew that joy was defined as 'a state of mind and an orientation of the heart.' Joy was also a 'settled state of contentment, confidence and hope.' It was something or someone that could provide a source of happiness. In the Bible in Jeremiah 31:13 it describesthe gift of joy: 'I will turn their mourning into gladness; I will give them comfort and joy instead of sorrow.' Proverbs 23:25 continues the expression of joy by saying, 'Let your father and your mother be glad, and let her rejoice who gave birth to you.'

I felt complete knowing the meaning of my birth name, as if by knowing, I'd received a direct thread to who I was and who I would become. Even without knowing its meaning I had followed the course I'd been given when my parents had named me Ilona. Joy had been a constant friend I'd discovered early on who'd helped me through my adversity. Joy had been a gift I freely gave to others. Joy had been mine from my birth.

When we understand the meaning of our name, we understand more of who we are, and who we can become. We embrace our truest, most authentic selves. We follow the path God laid out for us.

We discover our birthright.

Ilona Parunakova
Armenia, Ukraine, USA
International TEDx Speaker,
Doctoral Candidate in Christian Counseling and
PHD Christian Philosophy

Many Thanks

Many thanks to all who took the time to write their stories for this book.

The work has been a labor of love with the hope of inspiring, uplifting, and encouraging others as they face their own hard moments in life. I sincerely hope that any who are facing difficult times will find encouragement in the stories told here.

– Ilona

About the Author

Ilona is a descendent of survivors from the Ottoman genocide against the Armenian people during WWI. Whose great-great-grandparents were slaughtered before the eyes of her great-grandmother, who fled on foot as a child to escape. She herself witnessed the collapse of the Soviet Union and survived wartime in the Republic of Georgia immediately following, 1991-1993.

Ilona has additionally served with the Salvation Army as a Corps officer, liaison, writer, speaker, and as an organizer for fundraisers and other community events.

Ilona earned an Accomplishment and Achievement award in 2013 from the Salvation Army. She completed her Bachelor of Science degree in 14 months on an accelerated program to graduate summa cum laude with a 4.0 GPA. She is Integrative Nutrition Health Coach, Certified Personal Trainer, Certified Nutritionist and Certified NLP Master Practitioner.

She is proficient in English, Georgian, and Russian,

in addition to speaking some Ukrainian, Armenian, and Spanish. She is the author of Opium of the Almond Tree, a motivational memoir due to be released this fall by Gabriel's Horn. Ilona won People's Choice in a Republic of Georgia Beauty Pageant in 1998 and was chosen as the 2020 student speaker for Colorado Technical University. She has earned medals for completing a marathon and a triathlon. Please email ipschaal@icloud.com or visit IlonaParunakova.com